the making of a dragonfly

FOLLOWING CHRIST THROUGH THE WINDS OF CHANGE

MARY ETHEL ECKARD

LIFEWISE BOOKS

the making of a dragonfly
Following Christ Through the Winds of Change
MARY ETHEL ECKARD

Published by:

⚙ LIFEWISE BOOKS

PO BOX 1072
Pinehurst, TX 77362
LifeWiseBooks.com

Cover Design and Interior Layout and Design | Yvonne Parks | PearCreative.ca

To contact the author:
www.maryetheleckard.com

ISBN (Print): 978-1-947279-36-0
ISBN (Ebook): 978-1-947279-37-7

DEDICATION

To Aubrey, Kendall, Tyler and Patrick:
May the love of Christ shine in, around, and through you all the
days of your life.

SPECIAL THANKS

To my family and friends who prayed me through the eye of the
storm, gave me the grace of space, and never gave up on seeing this
dragonfly soar again. You are so loved.

TABLE OF CONTENTS

FOREWORD

Joy, joy, joy! My dearly beloved friend, Mary, asked me if I would consider writing a foreword to the book you are about to read. My response? A resounding, "Heck yes!" I couldn't be more thrilled or more frightened. I've never written a "foreword" before. Not wanting to mess it up, I Googled some suggestions on writing one and came away with the following:

1. Talk about the author *(duh)*. If you've been friends for many years, talk about the friendship. *Groovy—I love to talk about our friendship!*

2. Keep it light and fluffy. *I can do light and fluffy!*

3. Keep it short (between 750 and 1,500 words). *Yikes, now I'm stressing. I already used up 120!*

In an effort to keep this light and fluffy I thought I'd play a little game with you. It's called "Two Truths and a Lie." If you haven't played this game before don't worry—it's easy. If you don't like to play games—tough toenails. This is my foreword, so I get to call the shots. (Wink-wink—just teasing. You don't have to play, but if you would read along with us that'd be great).

The object of the game is this: I'm going to tell you three things about Mary. Two of the statements will be truths. One will be a lie. You win if you can correctly pick out the lie. Ready? Let's do this.

Three things about Mary:

1. God asked Mary to cough up her kidney for a neighbor in need of a transplant. She did as God requested but named her kidney "Ethel" before passing it along. She's been known to send "Ethel"—the kidney—birthday cards.

2. Mary worships dragonflies and even sprouted dragonfly wings on her back—just above her shoulder blades. Fortunately, her bra straps keep them in place so they don't come loose willy-nilly.

3. God gave Mary a vision for a ministry. He even gave her a piece of paper and a sharpened #2 pencil so she could write His instructions down. I guess He didn't think she could carry stone tablets like muscle-man Moses did.

The answer is… (drum roll, please). You know what? I'm not going to give you the answer after all. I'll keep you in suspense. You can discover the answer for yourself as you read this beautiful book, which, by the way, I've already read and completely loved because it's *so* Mary. What does "so Mary" mean? You will soon understand, so don't feel left out.

Onto our friendship—because we all know by now that a good foreword includes "friendship-talk." God brought Mary into my life nearly twenty years ago. We worked together in the corporate world in Dallas, Texas. Our desks were close to one another—as in "almost touching." Remember the old TV show "The Office" (2005-2013)? You get the picture.

I still think it's funny how God orchestrated our meeting. She was from South Carolina, with a precious accent. I was from New York, with a not-so-precious accent. Despite the differences, our hearts connected and amazing things began to happen. I was given the great gift of seeing Mary slowly transform before my eyes. She transformed from a woman who questioned God's love for her, to a woman who has become a truly amazing and anointed Christian speaker, teacher, and now author, too. I'd love to tell you about her journey of faith, but you will enjoy it more as she personally shares it with you in the pages that follow.

These pages are filled with her humor and humility. There are stories that will make you laugh out loud, and some that will bring you to tears because her stories are so relatable. This journey has encompassed the pains and joys of being a wife, a mother, a daughter, a sister, a friend, and above all servant to our Lord, Jesus Christ.

The first time I read this book, I closed it, and a beautiful verse from the Bible washed over me.

"O death, where is your victory? O death, where is your sting?" [1]

This is a song of triumph, a song that Mary knows by heart. If you need some encouragement, you will find it. If you are feeling lost, she will point the way. If you are reading these words now, then trust that God Himself has brought you here and He loves you with an everlasting love.

Enough of the heavy stuff and onto the book. What do you say we strap on our seatbelts and get ready for an amazing ride with Mary! The engine is revving—hop on board. You will be very glad you did!

Joyfully submitted by your friend in Christ-Jesus,

Patty Zemanick-Williams, a.k.a. "The Holy Roller"
Author & Friend

P.S. For the record, this foreword contains 820 words—just saying. (Wink-wink) To God be the Glory. Amen and amen.

Happy reading.

THIS BOOK AS A STUDY TOOL

In this book, *The Making of a Dragonfly*, Mary pours out her soul in a personal and precious account of her walk with our Lord. She has opened her heart to share painful memories, resistance, silence, depression, and fear. More importantly, she shows us that, through the most difficult times of her life, God draws her closer in to a secret and safe dwelling place, teaches her to walk with Him in obedience, and to seek only Him as her guide.

"He who dwells in the secret place of the Most High shall abide under the shadow of the Almighty." Psalm 91:1[1]

I can think of no better way to describe the journey that Mary shares with us in her book, *The Making of a Dragonfly*, than this scripture passage.

As you read each chapter, find a quiet place to make yourself vulnerable before God, to take the lessons that Mary shares, and personalize them. To get the most out of this book, I suggest using the journal pages at the end of each chapter to note places in your life that need more reflection, and areas where you want to draw closer to God. Mary has provided footnotes and scripture as well—do not miss these! The footnotes and scripture provide more insight into Mary's lovingly friendly personality, along with additional paths for a deeper dive into your individual journey. I encourage you to use this book as a devotional or study guide; it can be life changing for you, if you will open your heart and mind to the messages within.

Sandra Hammack,
Sister

DRAGONFLY SYMBOLISM

Dragonfly Ministries

The dragonfly is a symbol of growth and development. She is her strongest when she stays close to her source of strength, the sunlight. As she absorbs warmth from the sun, she reflects it through her wings for the world to see.

We are much like the dragonfly, created to grow and develop into all God has purposed for us. We are our strongest and best when we stay close to our source of strength, the SON light. As we absorb His light, His Holy Spirit teaches, guides, and shines through us so others are drawn to Him.

The dragonfly serves to remind us we too can reflect the light of Christ in a darkened world by letting His Son shine through us.

Will you be a dragonfly for God?

> *"For God, who said, 'Let light shine out of darkness,' made His light shine in our hearts to give us the light of knowledge of the glory of God in the face of Christ." 2 Corinthians 4:6*

INTRODUCTION

I am twice married; twice divorced. The first divorce was because I wanted out; the second was because he wanted out. The breakup of the second marriage is where my journey into brokenness and pain began and where God brought healing, wholeness and purpose. It has taken many years to understand how God makes beauty from ashes.[1] He pours healing into brokenness in a way that spreads to others who are amidst similar storms.

I write this book out of obedience, to honor the God whose process of walking me through this storm has honored me. This is a book of healing—not only for me, but for readers who face similar situations. It is imperative I share some views and events so others can recognize, learn, and heal from the experience of my pain and wounds.[2] Some chapters have been difficult to write and will be difficult for readers traveling a similar road. The hallmarks of healing are the same. We can walk through the healing of our deepest emotional wounds by allowing ourselves to "feel them out," or we can numb ourselves and hold onto the hurt. I have tried both. Numbing may last for a while, but true healing comes when we lay our numbing mechanisms aside and give God access to our heart wounds.

For those on a journey to inner wholeness, I pray for complete emotional, mental, and spiritual healing. I also pray for you to have greater understanding of those who are struggling in similar ways. I was carried through this journey under the shelter of His wings.[3] He will carry you, too. You are the apple of His eye,[4] and the things that concern you are of greatest concern to Him, for He is your Father.

My writing and teaching styles are the same. I write and speak of things God has taught me, yet each of these things are applicable to you as well. For instance, I share how God showed me I was living in a cage of fear, and how He rescued me. This story also applies to you. God will show you what your cage is—whether it's fear, lust, selfishness, etc. He will reveal what is holding you back from freedom, and He will teach you through my journey if you are open to learn. As you read, ask the Holy Spirit to guide you in applying these teachings and truths to your life.

I pray your faith in God will be multiplied, and I pray His promises forward in your situation. May seeds of love and restoration fall to the ground and present a harvest of hope and faith for those who walk through life's storms in God's way. Yes, Lord, You make all things new. Amen.

Finally, God blessed me with an amazing family to walk me through this season of learning. My children and grandchildren have provided the oil of gladness on days I didn't know if I would survive. My church staff believed in me, helped me find my voice, and loved me back to wholeness. And to you, my sisters, friends, ministry partners, and dragonflies who kept the faith, prayed, stayed in touch, and loved me and my family—a large thank you and hootie-hoo!

> *"May these words of my mouth and this meditation of my heart be pleasing in Your sight, Lord, my Rock and my Redeemer."*
> *Psalm 19:14*

CHAPTER 1

THE STORY UNFOLDS

"Before I formed you in the womb I knew you, before you were born I set you apart." [1]

MY SOUTHERN UPBRINGING

I am Mary Ethel Eckard, named after both grandmothers, Mary and Ethel. Typical to southerners, I was called Mary Ethel through the fourth grade. In middle school, I realized other girls were called by one name, so I made the decision to be known as Mary Eckard. Not that it mattered. I lived in the same hometown and attended school with the same people my entire school life, so even though I tried to shorten my name, it didn't stick. I would still hear echoes of "Mary Ethel" as I walked through the school hallways, the neighborhood, or downtown streets.

I was raised in a Christian home in the small town of York, South Carolina, under the Southern Baptist tradition. My parents made sure their four children were surrounded by church, family, activities, and friends and understood Christian values and Biblical teachings. We had family devotions and prayer, attended church services three times a week, and were involved in youth programs, choir, and mission trips. We were loved by both parents and had the blessing of being surrounded and loved by aunts, uncles, cousins, and grandparents.

In addition to our involvement in our local church, dad was bass singer in a southern gospel quartet. The quartet had a tour bus, and we spent many weekends traveling to area churches, being part of the "gospel singings."

Because of the constant exposure to the gospel of Jesus Christ, I had no doubt God created the world in seven days. Nor did I doubt Jesus Christ was His Son who died for my sins. I invited Him into my heart at age eight. But even before that, I can't remember a time I was not aware of His presence.

YORK'S JUNIOR MISS

Growing up in a small town comes with little privacy. Not only did I know the names of my classmates and where they lived, I knew the owners of the drug store, the clothing store, and the managers at the department stores. It was hard getting into trouble because the small-town eyes were always watching; it was also difficult keeping a secret—which brings me to share the story of how I became a beauty queen. (I have never been a beauty queen.)

The summer before my senior year, I was thumbing through our local newspaper, *The Yorkville Enquirer*, when I came across an article inviting contestants to compete in the S.C. Junior Miss Pageant.

I wrote a letter to the board of judges expressing an interest in competing. To my surprise, they sent an application and asked me to complete and return it with a recent photo. I had a telephone interview with two of the judges. Several weeks after the interview, I was invited to a local venue where I would be crowned York's Junior Miss. Wait. What? No competition? No parading of contestants to choose the best candidate? No probing questions to test my worldview knowledge? For the cost of two postage stamps, I stepped into the world of celebrity and fame. (That's overstated quite a bit.)

At the crowning venue, I was presented as York's Junior Miss and received my tiara. It didn't dawn on me the other girls present and receiving their titles and tiaras had been selected in much the same way; otherwise they would have been crowned at their hometown competition.

Back to the difficulty of keeping a secret in a small town. Because I was embarrassed at the way it all came about, I didn't want anyone to know about my newfound celebrity. But my dad was senior pressman for the hometown newspaper and close-knit with the writers and reporters, so I made the weekly news, complete with a photo and article about the upcoming S.C. Junior Miss Pageant.

After the newspaper article, a girlfriend asked, "Who did you compete against to be named York's Junior Miss?" When she heard my muted answer, she laughed hysterically and responded, "Great accomplishment!" I surmised that when you're the only one competing, chances of winning are pretty high. Needless to say, I had lots of competition in the state pageant. I'll leave it at that, for now.

THE CALL FOR "THE ALL"

After graduating high school, I sensed God's call to ministry in these two words, "Follow Me." I didn't tell anyone how God was leading me; it was private. And besides, I was not interested in traveling overseas or working in a church; in my limited thinking, those were the only two options. My personality is to go all-in when I do something, and I knew answering the call affirmatively would most likely put me in the dimension of being labeled a Jesus freak. The Christian life, as I understood, was about what one did for Jesus and for others to see. I did not yet grasp the truth that the Christian life is more a heart issue than an outward issue. My response was, "Not now."

I had a plan for my life, and my plan seemed much more appropriate than God's. My plan was to be a wife and mother and own a house. Looking back, I see how shortsighted those plans were, but then, the dreams seemed to be the height of life's fulfillment.

The call to ministry was not easy to escape as I knew "not now" was not the answer that pleased God, and pleasing God would require all of me. I wanted to choose who had access to "the all." He could have a little, but "the all" belonged to me. After all, Christianity as I had experienced it seemed to contain more "shall-not's" than "shall-do's."[2]

THE SEED OF REBELLION

Dad called me a live wire because of my energy level and love of adventure. He also called me stubborn, because I would fight for what I wanted. Both traits have followed me through life, sometimes in ways honoring to God but more often in ways for selfish promotion and desires.

**Stubbornness paired with pride
nourishes the seed of rebellion.**

In rural southern towns, it was typical for girls to marry immediately after graduation and start families. After completing business school, I married my high school boyfriend and soon became mom to two beautiful daughters. We purchased our first home and just like that, my life's dreams were realized. But rather than achievement, I was filled with emptiness, still fighting the call of God. As much as I loved and adored the daughters, they could not fill the hole in my heart. I reached out to God and He met me, eager to fill my emptiness, but the realization He still wanted all of me angered me and sent me back into me-mode.[3] I didn't want the life God had for me; it felt too restrictive. I wanted to live life my way with His blessing. (My way with His blessing was a trap that tightened its grip over my life for many years beyond this point.)

After a few years, the marriage hit a low point, with both partners headed in different directions. I chose to walk away from the marriage, not considering the pain or destruction divorce would bring into the life of my husband or daughters.

With newfound freedom, I wanted to explore the life of being single and discover what had been missed by marrying young. To escape small town gossip and prying eyes, I relocated the daughters to a new city and enrolled them in new schools. I worked two jobs to make ends meet and made decisions I had no business making. Still, I was constantly aware of God's presence and His call to return to Him.

At one point during the legal separation, I second-guessed my decision to divorce and quietly laid a fleece[4] before God. In the Bible, Gideon lacked confidence in God's promise of victory, so he asked God for a sign, using wool fleece, to confirm the promise. After God confirmed the promise, Gideon asked for a second sign, again demonstrating his lack of faith and God's confirmation of faithfulness. At this season in life, I had not learned completely to discern God's voice. I knew

He was for marriage, but I also knew it wasn't something I wanted. Through this Bible story, I learned to lay questions before God and ask Him for a sign to demonstrate His answer and His will.

In my fleece, I asked, "Lord, if it is Your plan for me to return home to my husband, please let him randomly show up at the door and ask me to come home." That night, my husband came to the apartment and asked me to come home. I knew God sent him, but without hesitation, I slammed the door in his face. That was not the answer I wanted when I asked for God's help. It was at that point I completely turned my back on God. I didn't know what I wanted out of life for the long-term, but for the short-term, living the single life was at the top of the list. No one was going to deter me from getting what I wanted—not even God. (I cringe at my transparency and the truth in this statement. I further cringe when I see how this decision brought year upon year of pain and isolation to my family.)

Self-centered living leads to mistakes, regrets, broken homes and broken relationships that may take a lifetime to unravel and heal. The decisions made today feed our lives tomorrow, and decisions build upon decisions. Messes are made and cleaning up those messes takes time. From church and God to worldly living and thinking, a taste of sin can derail a life for many years. It takes an intervention of God to get a life lived through selfish eyes and prideful heart back on track.

My self-centered and carefree lifestyle was a train wreck as I sought happiness in people and relationships rather than in Christ.

I buried my head in the sand, ignored the truth, and walked away from the destruction as though it never occurred. The "glamor" of the single life lasted about two years before I woke up to reality. I was derailed, and sin revealed the darkness within my heart. I was in a miserable mess and began looking for a way out, a rescue.

Because of my lifestyle, I didn't look to God as my rescue. I understood God's plan for my life had not changed, and He wanted all of me. I was not ready to surrender to His plan nor was I interested in changing who I was. I controlled my life. Mistakes had been made, but I could fix things myself. I didn't need God to enter and rearrange anything. I had this.

So, I did what I knew to do. I looked for a good man to pull me out of my darkness and help me get back into the light.

FOLLOWING CHRIST

Write the Bible reference or quote from this chapter you would like to research.

Reflections: (Reflect on what resonates with you from this chapter.)

Focus Areas: (Where do you see areas to draw closer to God?)

Actions: (What will I do this week based on my focus areas?)

Prayer: (Pen a prayer to God, inviting Him into this area of your life.)

CHAPTER 2

FOREVER HUSBAND

*"'Return to Me,' declares the Lord Almighty, 'and
I will return to you.'"* [1]

MY RESCUE

My rescue came when I met my "forever husband." We were friends
before dating and dated a year before marriage. He was also raised
in a Christian home and appreciated my Christian background and
values. He loved me and cared for my daughters; he was a good
provider, and he was the answer to my woes. The marriage vows
were spoken from the depth of my heart. He rescued me, and out of
gratitude, I vowed to devote my life to serving him as a good wife.
The daughters and I relocated to be with him and began our lives
anew in North Carolina.

With the purchase of a home, my life dream was again realized. Yet the spiritual loneliness was deeply rooted in my heart, and no amount of striving or reaching out to forever husband could fill the void. In addition, our emotional wounds and immaturity had remained hidden long enough to win one another, but the stress of relocating, marriage, new work, and schools began to tear away the layers of our outer shells, exposing characteristics of stubbornness, insecurity, and pride.

Our first year of marriage was riddled with arguments and disagreements. We loved deeply and fought passionately. By God's grace, we survived the chaos and adjustment of seeing the exposed people we truly were. We slowly began to accept each other's faults and weaknesses and settled in to married life with children.

I knew the solution to my heart problem would only be found in Christ. As I stated earlier, He had been my constant companion in childhood, and the emptiness had begun when I slammed the door on Him at the breakup of the first marriage. But how could I expose my spiritual brokenness to forever husband? In our early days, he pointed out those believers passionate for God and labeled them Jesus freaks, talking about how they were over the top in their display of faith. I feared when he learned of my hunger and thirst for God, he would reject me for being a one-dimensional Jesus freak wife. Satan's deceptive words whispered that forever husband would not share me with God, so I needed to hide the truth. I desired to love both God and forever husband, but I didn't know how to elevate one higher than the other. So, in my heart, they shared the throne.

This deception and fear produced a mindset of serving two masters.[2]

Our marriage eventually put us back in church, where we dedicated our lives to following Christ. The daughters received salvation and were baptized. They spent every spare moment immersed in the church youth program, and I moved slowly into ministry, trying to leverage my commitment between God and forever husband. After a while, we became the parents of two sons, born two years apart, who were the pride and joy of forever husband's heart (and mine as well). Our home was full and our family complete.

RELOCATION TO TEXAS

After several years of marriage, the job relocated us from North Carolina to Texas. Our marriage had survived the early years, and we were excited about the new adventure. Our house sold quickly, we found the perfect home in Texas for our family of six, and we transplanted our lives again. We quickly developed friendships within the Texas community and became involved in church ministry.

There was only one problem.

I had not shared with forever husband (or anyone else) my spiritual hunger for God, nor the call to ministry. Our marriage had not been built on the true foundation of Christ. We had jumped into marriage without fully understanding each other's spiritual background and desires. We had never discussed Christ at a deep level; we both assumed we had the same understanding of Christianity, and we did not regularly attend church together until after we were married.

The emptiness in my spirit was not quenched by forever husband, nor by my children, nor by work or church or community. From the onset of our marriage, forever husband was supposed to be the light in my darkness, but I realized my heart longed for more. There was a great hunger to know God and an even greater awareness that as hard as I tried to live rightly, my life was stained with past and present sin. This problem, intertwined with the lie of Satan that forever husband would not love a one-dimensional Jesus freak,[3] had me nailed to the ground.

Satan's deception can lead us off track. Exposing lies and countering them with the truth is the best way to shut down the deception. Had I shared with forever husband my passion for Christ at the onset of our relationship, decisions and adjustments would have been made early in our relationship, rather than staying hidden through years of marriage and exposed in destructive ways.

I wanted to serve Jesus more, but I didn't want forever husband to oppose me because of my one-dimensionality. I did what I knew to do. I went into internal mode, not sharing my thoughts or fears with forever husband. In one of my darkest moments, I was looking for the light and leaving him in the dark of my struggles.

Privately, I began searching scripture. I knew God had forgiven my past sins, but I couldn't shake the day-to-day attitudes, motives, and habits that seemed to have control. My mind and heart were reflected in the words I spoke.[4] I had issues with gossip, worry, complaining, entitlement, discontentment, pride, and self-centeredness. I still wanted things my way and was not able to appreciate what God graciously provided. I felt it would take not only a stump grinder but a root buster to remove all the ugliness in my heart. "Lord, please show me how to move from sin into peace; from selfishness into love."

PSALM 51 PRAYER

One morning, I paused while reading this raw and powerful plea for forgiveness and cleansing:[5]

"My sin is always before me. Cleanse me with hyssop, and I will be clean; wash me, and I will be whiter than snow. Create in me a pure heart, O God, and renew a steadfast spirit within me."

This was the cry of my heart. I implored God to transform my stubbornness into perseverance and my pride into humility. I asked Him to return me to the pure heart of my youth when I trusted and lived for Him. As the days and weeks passed, I asked God to make Himself known to me so I could understand who I was through His eyes. I sought assurance God was still available to me.

I feared I had messed things up so badly I would only be allowed to stay on the sidelines of His plan rather than be in the limelight of His love.

The things of God I had pushed away for years were now the desires of my heart. I didn't understand that God had planted His desires deeply within my heart, and my prayers were reflecting His thoughts. Something inside me was changing. Christianity was becoming my inner life. I wanted my heart to be more like Jesus. The inner life needed to grow so the outer life would be a result of what was happening inside, not something I strived to produce from my own strength.

When we pray in accordance with God's will, our prayers will be answered.[6] God did not disappoint. His answers came in unexpected ways, on unexpected days, and through unexpected people.

Lord,

Create in me a pure heart. Forgive my rebellion, selfishness, and pride. Give me the desire to be all You have created me to be. Open my eyes to see you, my heart to love you, my ears to hear you. Come back as my constant companion. Heal me and remove my fear of being all You have created me to be; remove my fear of being nicknamed a one-dimensional Jesus freak. Amen.

FOLLOWING CHRIST

Write the Bible reference or quote from this chapter you would like to research.

Reflections: (Reflect on what resonates with you from this chapter.)

Focus Areas: (Where do you see areas to draw closer to God?)

Actions: (What will I do this week based on my focus areas?)

Prayer: (Pen a prayer to God, inviting Him into this area of your life.)

CHAPTER 3

UNEXPECTED WAYS,
DAYS, AND PEOPLE

*"As the heavens are higher than the earth, so are my ways
higher than Your ways and my thoughts than Your thoughts."* [1]

THE HOLY ROLLER

While in Texas, I worked in the corporate world with Patty,[2] a
woman of high accomplishment and high energy. She worked
in the legal department, which housed rows of file cabinets. One
evening, unbeknownst to Patty and for aesthetic purposes, the
legal department had the file cabinets relocated to the far end of
the building. The next day Patty wasted much time in the retrieval
of files because of the distance between the legal office and the file
cabinets. She went home for lunch and came back wearing roller

blades.[3] It would have been a great idea had Patty known how to use the skate brakes but delivering files to an attorney by using their desk as a braking mechanism was frowned upon. The next day when she arrived at work, the file cabinets were back in their original location, and the roller blades were put away.

Patty was also a great storyteller and communicator. She had a passionate love for God and the ability to see His handiwork in the smallest of details. She shared stories of how she sensed God's presence during her morning commute, through a conversation with a neighbor, in a sunrise or sunset, or in nature. She also had the ability to discern God's voice and shared conversations between her and Heavenly Father. I was envious of her relationship with God. Why could she hear His voice and discern His promptings and I could not?

**Her never-ending stories and passion for Him
fueled the desire burning within me to know
Him more.**

Patty also embodied the gift of persistence in wanting others to know God intimately. In fact, when Patty returned home to upstate New York years later, the priest called her a "holy roller" because she asked to start a women's Bible study within the first few weeks of her arrival. God used Patty's passion and persistence to redirect many lives, including mine.

One morning at work, Patty stepped into my comfort zone and said, "I'm leading a Bible study at my church. It's called *Experiencing God*,[4] and I want you to come." I responded, "I'm too busy" (I wasn't). She ignored my invitational decline and continued, "It's about learning to recognize God's voice. It is life-changing, and you are going to do the study with me." Again, I declined the invitation by insisting,

"No, I'm not!" (I really wasn't). She moved on to the next topic of discussion, so I thought I had won the battle. But at the end of the day, she waved goodbye while shouting over her shoulder, "See you tonight. The study starts at seven."

Under obligation, I attended the study to get her off my back. I had been praying for humility, but I didn't dream God would take my independent nature and make me dependent on other people for spiritual growth. In God's divine wisdom, He used both Patty and the study to open my heart to His voice and humble me to learn from others.

THE FOUR-YEAR-OLD

The same time this study began, I met a four-year-old named Johnston. He lived two doors down. The commute from his house to ours was less than a minute, but even with his little four-year-old legs, he could traverse the route in under ten seconds. Talk about a live wire and a ball of energy! He could run circles around me, the sons, and even the dog. For some reason, God thought I needed high-energy people to get my attention. First Patty, and now Johnston. And the timing of these two people in my life was not coincidental.

I first met Johnston on the sidewalk outside our home. Our daughter Kendall was leaving for her high school prom when he caught sight of her and raced up the sidewalk. He asked if he could touch her dress, and with these eight words he won our hearts, "I have never seen a real princess before."[5]

It was not uncommon for Johnston to ring the doorbell and ask to play with the sons. Often, he climbed onto the bar stool and talked to me as I prepared dinner. As I cooked, he shared exciting tidbits from his four-year-old perspective and told me stories about his day.

His imagination was active, his aspirations were larger than life, and on some days, he enjoyed conversing with me more than playing with the sons. He was inquisitive and talkative. One of my favorite questions revolved around family dinner. If there were only enough place settings for our family, he would ask, "Ms. Mary, where is my plate?" He became a much-loved staple in our family and a welcomed dinnertime guest.

A NEW KIDNEY

After meeting Johnston's family, I learned his mom was on a waiting list for a kidney transplant. Her illness was a private matter and not a casual discussion topic with strangers. She was managing life while waiting for a cadaver kidney. She was not frail, nor was she a victim. She was courageous and heroic, doing what needed to be done without drama, complaint or fanfare. She worked full-time, had her dialysis treatments during non-work hours, and kept her family and household going.

Because of my love for Johnston, I wanted to understand more about kidney disease and how it affected his family. I hesitantly approached his mom to voice my questions and concern about her condition and dialysis treatments. She graciously invited me to accompany her to see firsthand what dialysis involved. After witnessing the withdrawal, cleansing, and replacement of her blood by a machine, I began to understand the difficulty of enduring this process three sessions a week, four hours each session. I read pamphlets about dialysis and the way it affects the internal organs and taxes the body. It seemed hopeless, yet here was Johnston's mom, doing what had to be done to stay in the game of life with no complaints. She understood the gift of dialysis was keeping her alive, and rather than being bitter about her circumstances, she was grateful for each day.

A few days afterward, something happened that joined the Johnston and Patty puzzle pieces. Suddenly it made sense. God had put me in the *Experiencing God* course so I could learn to recognize His voice and promptings. At the same time, He introduced me to a four-year-old who won my heart with his personality and limitless energy. It seemed I was being presented with a divine opportunity. I sensed the Lord say, "I brought you from North Carolina to this home to gift a kidney to Johnston's mom." The vision was a beautifully wrapped box with the gift of life inside. My first reaction was excitement; my second was doubt.

Questions flooded my mind. Did God ask me to donate a kidney to someone I barely knew, or was my love for Johnston trying to fix what was broken? Would forever husband support surgery to benefit someone he had met once? How was I to discern between my big heart and God's voice?[6]

Only God had these answers. So again, I laid out a fleece[7] in search of an answer. "Lord, if this is You, I need confirmation. To move forward, I need the blessing of forever husband. He is protective of me. I don't know how to broach the topic. He will have questions and need assurance my health is not at risk. Please give me the answers he needs. If this is Your voice, please let him give his blessing."

I tried to research, but being a living donor was uncommon,[8] and there wasn't much information available. In addition, the medical community believed family members were the best fit. It seemed I was blocked at every turn. With limited information, I approached forever husband and explained what God had placed on my heart. I asked for his blessing to proceed in seeing if Johnston's mom and I were a match. He asked the questions I was prepared to answer. There was tenderness in his eyes and tone of his voice as he responded,

"If God has asked you to do this, who am I to stand in the way?"

When forever husband gave the green light, I knew God intended to heal Johnston's mom. The next hurdle would be convincing her to accept the gift. She was skeptical that I would be a match and didn't want to waste our time for negative results. But having learned from Patty, I persisted until she relented. Three months of medical exams, interviews, and tests were completed. Finally, the call came. "The test results are in and it's a miracle. It's as if you are sisters; it could only be a closer match if you were identical twins." Johnston's mom would soon have a kidney, and her days of dialysis would be no more.

A NEW HEART

God was working overtime to answer my Psalm 51 prayer. He was changing my prideful heart to a teachable heart. He opened the door with the kidney transplant to help me communicate about spiritual things with forever husband. And He was building my trust. On the day of surgery, the thought came to mind, "What if I don't wake up? What about forever husband and our children?" But I knew God had called me and would guard me. Even if His plan involved taking me to heaven, He would provide for my family. My faith was indeed stretched and increased.

The doctors said the kidney began working before it was sewn in. Johnston's mom said she felt better than she had in years. Her first words to me after surgery were, "Thank you for giving me back my life." She accepted and received God's beautifully wrapped gift! As for me, I witnessed a miracle. God gave Johnston's mom a new kidney, and at the same time, He gave me a new heart—a heart bent toward obedience.

NEIGHBORHOOD IMPACT

The entire neighborhood seemed to be involved in the kidney story. Cards and flowers were delivered to the hospital and to our homes. News crews, reporters, and cameras bombarded the hospital and neighborhood to capture the before, during, and after stories. There were cameras and reporters in the surgery rooms that recorded the transplant of the kidney from one body to the other. Our friend surprised us by catering the hospital waiting room with food from local grocers so family members and friends would not have to leave their posts for sustenance. Even after surgery, Johnston's mom and I were invited to participate in an educational video to encourage other non-related donors to "cough up a kidney" as Patty would say.

UNEXPECTED WAYS, DAYS AND PEOPLE

In His unexpected ways, on unexpected days, and through unexpected people, God gained my full attention and showed me the life change that comes when we accept the call of obedience. Not only was my life impacted, but also the life of an entire community.

What else did He have in mind to further test this desire for an obedient heart? Would rebellion return or would faith prevail?

FOLLOWING CHRIST

Write the Bible reference or quote from this chapter you would like to research.

Reflections: (Reflect on what resonates with you from this chapter.)

Focus Areas: (Where do you see areas to draw closer to God.)

Actions: (What will I do this week based on my focus areas?)

Prayer: (Pen a prayer to God, inviting Him into this area of your life.)

CHAPTER 4

THE AFTERSHOCKS OF OBEDIENCE

"Whoever claims to live in Him must walk as Jesus did." [1]

Great movements and miracles of God are often accompanied by aftershocks. My spiritual immaturity shielded me from understanding how obedience often shakes the foundation of our lives. I count my ignorance as God's favor and grace. Had I the slightest inkling of what was on the horizon, my heart of obedience would have died in the rubble.

THE GREAT DIVIDE

Forever husband and I could not deny God's orchestration of the miracle, but we didn't know how to grow beyond that. Though we were both involved in the miracle, I was the one experiencing intimate communication and revelations from God, and he was hearing about the experiences through my storytelling.

**Life changing power comes when we sit with God
and allow Him to teach us personally.**[2]

The aftershock of obedience began to shake our marital foundation, exposing a divided road. One fork returned to life as usual, the other led to a deeper discovery of God, the road less traveled. I chose the road less traveled, wanting to know the miracle maker. My spiritual pace quickened, and I wanted forever husband to run with me, but that was not his desire, and as hard as I tried, I could not force spiritual growth on him. (Or anyone else, for that matter.)

Forever husband's wife was forever changed, and the aftershock was filling the marital road with debris difficult to ignore or navigate. It seemed easier to hide my spiritual insights than to vulnerably display them for possible criticism or ridicule. Communication with a strong, outspoken, opinionated man was not my forte. My inability to quickly formulate thoughts or opinions to defend myself or my discovery of God only frustrated him. Forever husband was losing interest in listening, so I became silent in sharing, choosing rather to lean into God.

CONSIDERING THE COST

As I continued to open my spirit in discovering God, my hidden heart issues became more apparent—more rubble from the aftershocks. Was this part of the journey on the road less traveled? No wonder there were few fellow travelers.

Each day brought new areas needing the cleansing, healing, or corrective work of the Holy Spirit. Issues dealing with control, entitlement, manipulation, wrong thinking, motives, and attitudes.

Poor decisions from the past haunted me as I remembered the solitude of rebellious living. I did not want to return to that empty and dark place. Why, suddenly, was I so aware of my brokenness and rebellion? Why were these heretofore normal behaviors highlighted as areas to be surrendered? Clearly, the first issue for resolution was my inability to trust God. Why were these issues surfacing, and what did God require of me?

Oswald Chambers writes, "There is only one thing God wants of us, and that is our unconditional surrender. When we are born again, the Holy Spirit begins to work His new creation in us, and there will come a time when there is nothing remaining of the old life. How are we going to get a life that has no lust, no self-interest, and is not sensitive to the ridicule of others? The only way is by allowing nothing of the old life to remain, and by having only simple, perfect trust in God—such a trust that we no longer want God's blessings, but only want God Himself."[3]

I wasn't sure what Mr. Chambers meant. In my limited experience, a heart of obedience meant enjoying the blessings of God. Was I to set aside the blessings of obedience and simply trust God, no matter the results? That sounded like work and uncelebrated effort. Was I interested in getting to know God at a deeper level, even when glamor and celebrity[4] were not promised? How about when people turned against me because they could not relate to my spirituality? Did surrendering to God hold the same attraction? Would my self-centeredness die so God could be elevated?

The cost was great,[5] and the answer was not immediate nor half-heartedly considered. After a twenty-year delay, God brought me full circle with a renewed call to follow Him. I wanted to give Jesus "the all," but I also knew there would be fallout of relationships. Full surrender would open me to ridicule, mockery, and separation from those who were not walking the same spiritual road. All things considered, I responded, "Yes, Lord."

In the blink of an eye, I stepped further into the zone of being sold out for Jesus, which I feared would eventually divide my marriage. But I did not discuss these things with forever husband, nor did I share my fears with him. Rather, I stored fear and hesitancy away in the recesses of my mind and asked God to deal with them. If my role was to follow Him, He could take on the responsibility of forever husband.

THE SECOND CHANCE

In tasting the love and activity of God during the kidney donation, my appetite cried for more of His presence. Was it possible He could take a mess like me and bring about a change? Would I humble under His care and see the true Mary behind the façade of cultural Christianity?[6] I wanted to live freely, reflecting His character from a place of devotion rather than a place of guilt and intentional striving.

I leaned into His Word and consumed scripture, hungry to understand more of this God who had called me to be His follower. As I read, I listed His attributes, characteristics, and promises. I was drawn into a pursuit of understanding this new way of thinking. "Lord, change me" became my heart's cry. With each day, it seemed I was more aware of my need for a complete makeover, from the inside out. I desired to walk in the original call of my life, to follow Him. Could it be possible to return to my original call? Then it happened—a second chance.

I received an invitation from a local church to speak at their annual women's conference, sharing my testimony of God's work during the kidney donation. Though appreciative of the opportunity, I was not excited about speaking in front of a group of women. Donating a kidney was one thing; it didn't require me to step outside my comfort zone, and besides, the doctors and media did all the work. This public speaking thing would require much of me; I would have to paint the picture of my story using my words. My introverted nature began to rise and scream "no." The enemy wasted no time taunting me with lies about my inability to effectively string words together to complete a thought, much less deliver a thirty-minute talk.

My mind raced back to the S.C. Junior Miss Pageant, which had been telecast to local audiences. Attired in my evening gown and tiara, I stood on stage with forty other girls in front of two hundred guests and a panel of judges. The talent portion had been nerve-wracking as I sang the song, "Let Me Be There," as recorded by Olivia Newton John.[7] Next, each girl was expected to answer a question about national or international news. Sure, Dad worked for the local newspaper, but that didn't mean I read it. Watching the television news was what you did when you only had one channel. I was lost and had an overwhelming sense of nausea and hopelessness. I wanted to run off stage and hide. So, I did what any smart girl does. I prayed to get a question where the answer, "world peace" made sense. I was not so lucky. I don't remember the question, but I remember the humiliation from the experience.

Now I was offered another chance to speak in pubic, in front of two hundred guests, and hopefully without a panel of judges or probing news questions. Could God possibly redeem the last fiasco and do something amazing? The temptation was to say "no," to run and hide, to return to life as usual rather than discovering God and who He created me to be. Just as with other decisions at this stage of life, I didn't answer quickly but took space to think, pray, reflect, and see if perhaps this was God's way forward. In the end, I knew the invitation was an opportunity to share the depth of God's love and hoped He would show up and help me do the talking.[8]

I prepared video news stories about the kidney donation as my introduction. I wrote out the story in complete paragraphs, 14-point font with highlighted words, and rehearsed until I was sick of myself. I asked God to give me the words to speak so I wouldn't look like a fool. I was self-consumed and a nervous wreck.

Then, as if by divine intervention, my prayers shifted to the audience, asking God to plant within each person a desire to know Him and hear His voice. When the prayer moved from self-interest to the spiritual growth of others, my nerves calmed, and I experienced God's peace. As I approached the podium, notes in hand, I sensed the calming of the Holy Spirit. As I shared my testimony of God's miracle, He rearranged my thoughts in such a way that I knew He spoke through me, taking my broken notes and weaving them into a story that touched those listening[9].

Stepping into this stretch increased my trust in God and opened my eyes to two treasured secrets. First, when we take on God's concern for others rather than bask in self-concern, we release our lives to be used of God and give Him responsibility for the outcome and results. Second, I became aware that somewhere in my destiny was a call to be a teacher and speaker. And I realized the thought of doing either of those two things made me want to go into hiding.

FOLLOWING CHRIST

Write the Bible reference or quote from this chapter you would like to research.

Reflections: (Reflect on what resonates with you from this chapter.)

Focus Areas: (Where do you see areas to draw closer to God?)

Actions: (What will I do this week based on my focus areas?)

Prayer: (Pen a prayer to God, inviting Him into this area of your life.)

CHAPTER 5

THE GIFT OF A DRAGONFLY

"The plans of the Lord stand firm forever, the purposes of His heart through all generations." [1]

GOD'S SILENCE

After the speaking engagement, God went into silent mode. Dead silence—as though He were the one hiding, leaving me to struggle through the fallout of my recent revelation. If He had truly destined me as a teacher and speaker, why was He silent? Was He playing a game? I needed life lessons, and I wanted them in my timing. Was I in timeout for something I was not aware of? In my childlike understanding of God and drawing from experience with people, I felt I was being punished by His silence and wondered if He had changed His mind about my purpose.

Oswald Chambers was a great help in explaining:

"God's silence is a sign that He is bringing you into an even more wonderful understanding of Himself. Are you mourning before God because you have not had an audible response? When you cannot hear God, you will find that He has trusted you in the most intimate way possible—with absolute silence, not a silence of despair, but one of pleasure, because He saw that you could withstand an even bigger revelation. If God has given you a silence, then praise Him—He is bringing you into the mainstream of His purposes."[2]

It would be many years before I understood the fullness of Mr. Chamber's wisdom and the way personal faith works *with* God's silence rather than against it. I was in God's school of "the wait," and silence was part of that preparation.

THE MAINSTREAM OF HIS PURPOSES

In scripture, we learn God sets apart those who desire to follow Him.[3] What does this mean? "To be set aside is to be rejected. To be set apart is to be given an assignment that requires preparation. In this set apart place, God gives special wisdom you will need for the assignment ahead. Look for the gift of being lonely. This will develop in you a deeper sense of compassion for your fellow travelers. And look for the gift of silence. This will allow you to hear God's whispers. This season is more about being prepared than being overlooked."[4]

Though I questioned being set apart, I sensed God had something in store and was choosing silence to teach me who He is apart from the activity of obedience. I knew He was preparing me for days ahead. I also knew with such preparation comes trials and opportunities to fail and succeed; to reject and to accept; to obey and to step back into rebellion. If silence was His way of preparing me for the journey, then I would lean into it and learn what He wanted to teach. My trust was small, but my faith was growing.

His silence, though disconcerting, became a challenge for me to press into rather than running back into rebellion.

BOYS, BUGS, AND BUTTERFLIES

Scripture portrays a God who continually pursues us.[5] He had pursued me and was holding me captive by His love. My pursuit was to understand how to fall more fully into His embrace and be given a new heart like His. But in addition to my ongoing pursuit of a silent God, I was involved in the day-to-day business of family. The daughters no longer lived at home, so my focus centered around helping the sons navigate life.

Boyhood was fun to observe. They had a "secret spot" at the back of our neighborhood where they escaped to play and explore with friends. Often, I would sneak through neighboring yards and hide behind shrubs to make sure they were safe and not messing with unauthorized property. I felt like spy-mama on a covert mission. They had other adventures as well; they drilled holes through their bedroom walls with screwdrivers to make peep holes for spying into the family room. They buried themselves in sleeping bags and slid down the narrow staircase. And they used their charm to delegate tasks to their mother. One such task involved bugs. Dead, smelly, crunchy bugs. Why bugs?

At the Dallas Zoo, our sons Tyler and Patrick discovered a trading post. They could collect items from nature and trade their collection for one donated by other children. The sons decided to put together an insect collection as their trade-in. The grandiose plan was to trade in dead bugs for a cool rock collection. Not surprisingly, I was part of their scheme to make the great exchange happen.

One evening before bedtime, Tyler asked, "Mom, when you're walking in the morning, will you get us some dead bugs?"

What would you say? How would you respond? "Dead bugs? No problem. I love picking up dead bugs and carrying them as I walk. It's Texas—it will give me somewhere to put my focus as I walk and sweat." Well, that's a little dramatic and Dr. Seuss-ish. My actual response was "Yep."

Dead bugs and prayer became the focus of my morning walks, not always in that order. After a few weeks of collecting, we glued butterflies and bugs to a foam board. (I later learned there are better ways to mount dead bugs to foam board—for example, pins designed specifically for that purpose). There was one space to be filled before the collection was complete. It looked like a great space for a dragonfly.

As I headed into the morning walk, I prayed to my silent God, who was apparently out of town on more important business. (Though a bit dramatic and untrue, I was a baby Christian at the time, learning who God is and making assumptions about Him drawn from human relationships.)

This time, I prayed out loud to make sure He heard. Maybe it was the silent praying that was the problem and not His disinterest in me.[6]

> *"Lord, if You love me, if You are real, if You truly have plans for my life other than coughing up a kidney, would You give me a dead dragonfly for this insect collection?"*[7]

He held His position of silence.

The next morning, I repeated the prayer, out loud, and searched with great expectation.[8] Again, silence. Not only were there no dead dragonflies, I had not seen one in flight. The absence of dragonflies was peculiar for a Texas summer day, as they were typically plentiful in the warmest months. My asking and God's silence were becoming the new norm, and I was growing frustrated. I had a mission from the sons and was not ready to give up. After all, my success equaled a trip back to the zoo.

GIFT OF A DRAGONFLY

On the third day, I pressed into the Lord again. My stubbornness was in the process of metamorphosing into perseverance[9] as I realized the discovery of a dragonfly for the collection was no longer the issue. My life seemed to hang in the balance of finding a dragonfly to confirm God's love, purpose, and plan. I desperately needed to know He had not used me for a kidney miracle and then tossed me into the disposal of uselessness.[10] I cried, "Lord, forgive me for the past. Remake me from the inside out. Please come back to me and show me Your love."[11]

I cannot explain how I went from the mountaintop experience of discovering God to the pit of despair so quickly. The loneliness in my spirit was filled to overflowing during the season of the kidney transplant, and now the emptiness fought to return. I battled to stay in the light of God's presence with a dark shadow hovering to overtake me and pull me back into the void.

On this morning walk, my vision was blurred by tears, and my head hung low, not wanting passersby to see my emotion. As a sprinkler system automatically started, I stepped off the sidewalk onto the curb, and history was changed. There, on the side of the road, braced against the curb, was a dragonfly, God's creation—broken and lifeless, just like me.

I gently gathered the insect, placed it into the zip lock bag, then held my head high and whispered, "thank you" to the heavens. I cried and giggled, danced and clapped my hands, not caring what passersby might think. My God was with me. He responded. I was not disposable; I was treasured. I was forgiven and loved! He had a plan and purpose for my life, and He had good things in store for me. He saw me. He knew me. He was real, and He loved me. He was real, and He loved ME!

My silent God waited three days to respond, so I would know it was His answer and not coincidence. He used those three days to show me what I valued and who He valued. He gave me the opportunity to lean into Him with expectation of His answer and affirmation of His love for me. He did all of this through two little boys who wanted to trade dead bugs and butterflies for a rock collection. My, how God continued to take puzzle pieces and put them into place to show me the picture of my life He had in store.

Little did I know, pressing into God for a dragonfly would redirect my life in ways I could not begin to imagine.[12] God was changing me from the inside out, transforming pride into humility, and revealing He was my teacher and mentor.

Forever husband and the sons had an earful that evening as I shared the dragonfly story, and the sons quickly started planning the next adventure to the Dallas Zoo.

FOLLOWING CHRIST

Write the Bible reference or quote from this chapter you would like to research.

Reflections: (Reflect on what resonates with you from this chapter.)

Focus Areas: (Where do you see areas to draw closer to God?)

Actions: (What will I do this week based on my focus areas?)

Prayer: (Pen a prayer to God, inviting Him into this area of your life.)

CHAPTER 6

FLASHBACKS AND AFFLUENCE

"As the rain and the snow come down from heaven, and do not return to it without watering the earth and making it bud and flourish, so that it yields seed for the sower and bread for the eater, so is my word that goes out from my mouth: it will not return to Me empty, but will accomplish what I desire and achieve the purpose for which I sent it." [1]

"THE WAIT" CONTINUES

My story of the dragonfly was shared with anyone who would listen, and often with those who didn't particularly care to hear. First there was the kidney story, now a dragonfly story. Was I really going to make a story out of everything that happened in life? Quite frankly, I was thrilled to have a story that involved something I was passionate about. With passion came the ability to speak in complete sentences with complete thoughts.

While others were talking about world events, sports, or neighborhood gossip, I immersed my interests in understanding spiritual things and seeing the handiwork and involvement of God. My world was turned upside down, and I couldn't function in the old way any longer. This road less traveled was lonely at times, but the scenery along the way was breathtaking. God had me, and I wasn't going to let Him go. I was on fire for the Lord and ready to get busy serving Him.

But He had me on hold. It was frustrating when He did not immediately put me on task or send me out. I couldn't manipulate, control, or influence the pace at which He moved, and He did not respond to my pleas of entitlement. Restlessness set in as I waited for ministry doors to open. I wanted the fast-track life of sharing Jesus, but God wanted to teach me about "the wait," which often feels like being in limbo. There were long days of waiting for something to happen, yet time had stopped.[2]

FLASHBACK REVELATION

I also struggled with loneliness. The daughters were out of the house, the sons were in school, forever husband was traveling, and my neighborhood girlfriend and I were having relationship struggles. How was it I had so few friends in Texas? There were women wanting to connect, yet I guarded my heart so heavily only a few entered. Through these questions, God revealed a deep emotional wound.

My mind traveled back to childhood. My first school friend came along when I was eight. When we were nine, we parted ways because she had a new friend and didn't need me anymore. The hurt of rejection set in, along with the conclusion friends would always leave me. This fear hovered throughout childhood as I hesitated to develop or nurture friendships and safely hid within the friendships made by church or family involvement—with one exception.

When I was twelve, I asked God for a best friend who would love me unconditionally, be my every day friend and school mate, and never leave me. I hoped God would hear the plea of a lonely little girl.

I saw her for the first time a year later. I was standing on the sidewalk outside the middle school, waiting for the homeroom bell to ring. She arrived with no fanfare, but to me, it was as though she came in on a parade float. I couldn't take my eyes off her. She was tall, thin, and beautiful with long blonde hair. As suddenly as she had appeared, she disappeared into the school office to get her class schedule. I looked for her throughout the day and found her at lunch, eating with a group of girls. Her name was Janice.

I believed her family had relocated from Jacksonville, Florida to York, South Carolina just for me. But she was the "new girl," and everyone was curious to know more about her, so I patiently waited my turn. As being a new student goes, she moved from group to group until finally she landed in my group of friends. It took less than a year before we were inseparable best friends. Everything I asked for in prayer was multiplied many times over as God bonded us heart, soul, and spirit. God brought Janice into my life at the age of thirteen, and many years later, our investment of love and time is still an ongoing cherished sisterhood and friendship. Traveling back in time helped me realize God's role in the orchestration of relationships. My friend Cheryl once told me,

"If you want to see God's faithfulness, look to your past."

If God answered my prayer in bringing Janice, I could trust Him to bring friends now.

"Lord, fill my days with friends. Remove this protective wall around my heart and help me be open to those You bring."

THE AFFLUENT WOMAN

One morning, I received a call from an affluent woman in our community. She had followed the kidney story, knew I was a Christian, and had a few questions. She was not from a Christian background and felt it important to understand Biblical history. She did not want to join a neighborhood Bible study that would expose her lack of knowledge. To prove her point, she added, "I don't even know who climbed the sycamore tree, was it Huckleberry Finn?" (It was Zacchaeus. The story is found in Luke 19:1-10.) She then asked if I would be willing to teach her the Bible, so she could "function in social settings."

Alas, this was the first invitation for my new surrendered life and the remedy for my restlessness and friendship issue. Was I willing to be stretched, to go into a home of affluence, expose my own lack of Biblical knowledge, and be open to someone who might eventually hurt and reject me? Clearly, this was an invitation from God indicating He had a new adventure in store.

I arrived at our first gathering to find five additional women wanting to gain Biblical knowledge within these prescribed guidelines:

- I was not to assign homework.
- It was not my job to convert them to Christianity.
- I was to cover topics, characters and events that might come up in social gatherings.

At our initial meeting, we discussed which study Bible to purchase and how to find a chapter and verse in scripture. Though written homework was not assigned, I stood on my book club soapbox and reminded them the best way to understand a book is to read it.[3] Several chapters of reading were assigned, beginning in the book of Genesis. I asked them to make a mental note of the characters, places, and events so we could review those the following week.

We gathered weekly for two years to discuss the assigned chapters. Yes, they had homework, and yes, we read and discussed the entire Bible. When we came to the book of John, one of the women shared, "I have been troubled as to why I do not hear God's voice. Our homework answered the question for me. It says, *"He who belongs to God hears what God says. The reason you do not hear is that you do not belong to God."*[4] After reading those words, I prayed and asked God to bring me into His family."

It wasn't my job to convict or convert them, but God used me as His vessel as He worked salvation in their lives, and He used the opportunity with these ladies to reveal my destiny of being a teacher of His words and His ways.

FOLLOWING CHRIST

Write the Bible reference or quote from this chapter you would like to research.

Reflections: (Reflect on what resonates with you from this chapter.)

Focus Areas: (Where do you see areas to draw closer to God?)

Actions: (What will I do this week based on my focus areas?)

Prayer: (Pen a prayer to God, inviting Him into this area of your life.)

CHAPTER 7

DRAGONFLY MINISTRIES

"Because of the Lord's great love we are not consumed, for His compassions never fail. They are new every morning; great is Your faithfulness." [1]

OVERWHELMED AND UNDERSTATED

I shared with forever husband the desire of the affluent woman and her friends to understand scripture in a safe place, starting with the basics. Again, God used forever husband to confirm next steps as he said, "I imagine there are people all over the world who feel the same way. You should start a website and post these lessons so others have a safe place to learn."

Forever husband's suggestion resonated with me, which was unusual. In our relationship, I typically pushed back on things forever husband suggested because it usually meant I did the work, and he supervised. In this instance, he offered to build the website and teach me the basics for maintenance. All he needed was the website name so he could purchase the domain and start building the pages. It's beautiful how God used forever husband to speak this website and ministry into life.

Even though he was offering to do the frontend work, I was overwhelmed with the scope of what was involved and paralyzed with fear. He suggested I write website studies, learn website software, and have a website name. His suggestions seemed understated as thoughts raced ahead to the responsibility of adding content, finding contributors, marketing, and being the face of the website. It was all too much. Besides, my destiny was to be a speaker and teacher, not a website guru or a writer.

The seed for a website had been planted in my mind, and I could not release the thought. My readiness to process forever husband's suggestion hit one autumn morning as I walked through a neighborhood under construction, so I began a conversation with God.

DRAGONFLY MINISTRIES

"Lord, what would You have me call this website?"

"Dragonfly Ministries"

"But Lord, that sounds so anti-Christian. How could that be a name that represents You?"

"I created the dragonfly."

"But Lord, why ministries instead of ministry?"

"Because there are more aspects of this ministry you will not understand until a future time."

As I walked I pondered these answers. These answers were not from me. I had no indication God would use the encouragement He gave me through a dragonfly to bring encouragement to people; let alone through a website. I also knew the dragonfly was a symbol in other cultures of good luck, and I didn't imagine God would want a ministry that would be linked to new age religion. And what did He mean He was giving me ministries? Clearly, He knew I was overwhelmed at the thought of managing a website and couldn't handle the capacity of whatever lay ahead.

PENCIL AND PAPER

"Lord, what do You mean 'ministries'? What lies in store?"

In my mind, I saw a diagram resembling a child's drawing of the sun. A circle in the middle with eight to ten sunbeams going out in all directions. The word "dragonfly" was written in the middle circle. The sunbeams started at the center of the circle and extended four inches straight, each going in a different direction. At the tip of the first sunbeam was the word "website." Then I saw words written at the top of each beam. I was overwhelmed. "Lord, You are showing me something I will not be able to remember. I need a pencil so I can write these things down."

I took three steps and found a no. 2 pencil with a freshly sharpened end. I whispered, "Thank You Lord. Now I need a piece of paper." Several houses up I spotted a construction site with a piece of yellow paper laying on the ground. The paper was from a yellow legal pad, dampened by the morning dew, but able to hold fresh lead. I placed the paper on top of a brick stack and quickly sketched the sunlight, sunbeams, and words from the vision.[2] I then dated the drawing, October 19–forever husband's birthday.

Rather than being overwhelmed by fear, I was encouraged. It was for a future time, and I was not to do anything more than write it down. Whatever God was asking of me in the way of a website was only the beginning of what He had in store. My task for the website was minimized when I saw His vision for the future.

DRAGONFLY SYMBOLISM

I raced home and began to research symbolism of the dragonfly. I found information about how dragonflies come to life and their maturation process. I read articles about the dragonfly lifespan and purpose in God's creation. I scanned stories of the way they reflect and refract the light from the sunshine. Sunshine? Hadn't God just given me the vision of sunlight and the beams that come from the sun? What was He trying to teach me through this small, beautiful creature and the sunlight? Was this another piece of my life puzzle?

As I poured through the information, I understood how the dragonfly represents our true self and penned the thoughts as the Holy Spirit gave them.

> The dragonfly is a symbol of growth and development. She is her strongest when she stays close to her source of strength, the sunlight. As she absorbs warmth from the sun, she reflects it through her wings for the world to see.

> We are much like the dragonfly, created to grow and develop into all God has purposed for us. We are our strongest and best when we stay close to our source of strength, the SON light. As we absorb His light, His Holy Spirit teaches, guides, and shines through us so

others are drawn to Him.

The dragonfly serves to remind us we, too, can reflect the light of Christ in a darkened world by letting His Son shine through us.

My desire is to be a dragonfly for God!

FULL CIRCLE AND FAITHFULNESS

After twenty years, I returned full circle to the call to follow Christ. The surrender to that call brought life change and direction. Decisions made in the years of selfish and rebellious living had to be worked out. Attitudes of the heart had to be purified. The courting stage of being with God and being remade by Him was just beginning. He had my undivided attention and devotion. I began to lean into Him during "the wait." Going ahead proved to be futile and mess making.

He taught me the importance of recognizing restlessness as a temptation to run ahead.

The lessons required trust in a Heavenly Father who is always working behind the scenes, is often silent in "the wait," and who does not feel the urgency in getting things done in my timing.

> "A quiet spirit is of inestimable value in carrying on outward activities; and nothing so hinders the working of the hidden spiritual forces, upon which, after all, our success in everything really depends, as a spirit of unrest and anxiety. There is immense power in stillness and all things come to him who knows how to trust and be silent."[3]

Slowly, I released the penmanship rights of my life to God, allowing Him to write my story. The events of the past year were falling into place. Experiencing God had opened my understanding to the ways

God speaks. The kidney donation had opened my senses. Friendship with the affluent woman had revealed a lifelong fear. The dragonfly had opened my spirit. God had used many puzzle pieces to bring these stories to life. What was next?

FOLLOWING CHRIST

Write the Bible reference or quote from this chapter you would like to research.

Reflections: (Reflect on what resonates with you from this chapter.)

Focus Areas: (Where do you see areas to draw closer to God?)

Actions: (What will I do this week based on my focus areas?)

Prayer: (Pen a prayer to God, inviting Him into this area of your life.)

CHAPTER 8

THE COURTSHIP OF GOD

"Your word is a lamp to my feet and a light for my path." [1]

THE COURTSHIP OF GOD

"Therefore, I am now going to allure her; I will lead her into the desert and speak tenderly to her. There I will give back her vineyards and will make the Valley of Achor (Trouble) a door of hope. There she will sing as in the days of her youth, as in the day she came up out of Egypt." [2]

My Heavenly Father allured me with His voice, His miracle, His presence. He used the loneliness and emptiness in my spirit to draw me. Every event, whisper, and occurrence He brought pulled me closer and planted within me the desire to step more fully into Him.

God was the new love of my life. He was center stage and taking the lead role on the throne; no longer should I serve two masters as I grew to understand my true worship belonged to God alone. (I was in love with forever husband but no longer could I allow my love for him to overshadow my love and worship for God. Though I desired to choose God, the struggle between the two masters would continue for a long season.)

I looked for God everywhere; I spoke to Him often. When I asked, He answered. When I cried, He comforted. When I was lonely, He was my companion. It was as though He were courting me, to show me His goodness and to win my whole heart into a lifetime commitment. I longed to experience and understand every aspect of God and to allow Him to work out His destiny in my life. How could I move forward in knowing Him at an even deeper level?

The answer came from the *Experiencing God* study. To know God is to experience Him; to experience Him is to become familiar with His ways. To understand His ways is to delve into the reading, study, and application of scripture.

This was a perfect fit. The affluent women's Bible study group was still going strong, and I spent days in preparation for each week's study, finding treasures on every page. I prayed, "Lord, give me a mentor to walk me through scripture." His response: "I am your mentor." I rephrased, "Lord, give me a teacher to show me things that will enhance my understanding." His response: "I am your teacher."[3]

The tradition of my upbringing had settled some things in my spirit that needed to be unlearned and retaught by the Holy Spirit. In my development years and early adult life, I had taken what others taught about the Bible and God's ways at face value. I had a secondhand knowledge of God, His ways, and His truth.

**I was hungry for a firsthand knowledge and the
need to be taught personally by the Holy Spirit.**

I was done with the outside voices bringing influence or twisting scripture. By digging in and researching scripture, God's truth was deposited into my mind and heart. Scriptures surrounded me at times of distress or when questions would arise.

I began practicing being alone with God, getting past the awkwardness of the silence and stillness and learning to sit in His presence, asking questions of the Bible, and searching scripture to find the answers. God had me in a quiet place, and now He taught me, one on one, about Himself. In the aloneness, I learned to be still, to wait, to lean into Jesus as companion, and to practice solitude, to recognize stillness in my heart and begin to understand contentment.

I took Him at His word that He would teach and mentor me. As I pondered scripture, I asked, "What does this scripture mean and how does it apply to life?" He taught me in very practical ways by using life's circumstances. He became my personal teacher. It was as though He were sitting with me, explaining scripture as I read. I wanted more.

I learned to recognize God's teaching in additional ways. Sometimes a partial Bible verse would pop into my mind, so I referenced the Bible to find the verse and see how it applied to my circumstance. Other times I would recognize repeating themes, words, names, items, numbers, phrases, etc. and reference scripture to find the Bible verse God was applying. I would read each referenced scripture until I found the one that resonated with my spirit. It's as though He were highlighting the scripture for me to see.

Here are a few stories and examples:

APPLYING SCRIPTURE IN CIRCUMSTANCES

In these early days of courtship, family funds were tight, and my clothes were worn as the children's needs took precedence over my outward appearance. One day I was walking along a farm road, thinking of an upcoming social event, not wanting to concern forever husband with my perceived vanity. I prayed, "What am I to wear to this engagement?" The Holy Spirit responded with a view of a field of wildflowers, and I sensed Him speak, "See the lilies of the field?"

I found the Bible reference about lilies. It read, ""Why do you worry about clothes? See how the lilies of the field grow. They do not labor or spin. Yet I tell you that not even Solomon in all his splendor was dressed like one of these. If that is how God clothes the grass of the field… will He not much more clothe you?"[4]

That evening, forever husband brought home an unexpected bonus and suggested I use it to buy a new outfit. God worked out the answer to my vain concerns before I asked. Through a phrase, God directed me to scripture to show His faithfulness in provision. Through forever husband, He provided the resources to clothe me in the splendor of Solomon.

APPLYING SCRIPTURE IN RELATIONSHIPS

Whether in the car or house, on the radio or in church, the same song held me. The lyrics sang of God as my hiding place, my safe place, my protector from the raging storms.

One evening, an acquaintance spoke words that made me feel small, embarrassed, and insignificant. As I drove home from the gathering, the radio played "my" song. Was God using this song to speak comfort?

I searched for the phrase "hiding place" and found this verse: "You are my hiding place; You will protect me from trouble and surround me with songs of deliverance."[5] God used this song to surround me with His love and protection and to again remind me He is always in front of me, preparing the way, and offering His love at every turn.

APPLYING SCRIPTURE IN OBEDIENCE

One weekend, our family traveled to the Carolinas for a visit. As we boarded the plane, I was relieved when forever husband sat with the sons on the opposite side of the aisle. I was window side next to a woman who spoke broken English. I was relieved because I didn't want to chat.

The first part of the trip was relaxing. The second part, my heart rate elevated as I heard a gentle prompting, "Place your hand on her and pray." I ignored the prompting and the racing heart. Again, "Place your hand on her and pray." I said, "But Lord, I don't know her, and she will think I'm crazy." Still He persisted.

I gently placed my finger on her sweater and quietly prayed. She gave no indication she felt my touch nor knew what I was doing. As I removed my finger, I heard the same prompting, not quite as gentle. "Place your hand on her and pray so she knows what you are doing. Don't be ashamed. Trust Me."

Clearly, I didn't trust, but His prompting pushed me into obedience. His ways are not our ways, and I remembered scripture, "Trust in the Lord with all your heart and lean not on your own understanding."[6] I placed my arm through hers and said, "The Lord wants me to pray for you." She nodded and closed her eyes. I moved my lips near her ear and began to whisper a prayer.

As I prayed, she wept. She wept the remainder of the flight. When we arrived at our destination, she hugged and thanked me. Even with the language barrier, she knew God met her 30,000 feet in the air and used a somewhat obedient woman to minister to her. The hidden story is how our son Patrick responded. As we waited at baggage claim, he said, "Mom, I saw what you did for that woman. When you prayed, she cried. That was a good thing to do."

God used a gentle prompting to direct me in trusting Him even when I did not understand His ways. He used the same prompting to touch the heart of a hurting woman and my young son. He is trustworthy and is always working in ways we do not know.

APPLYING SCRIPTURE IN REPENTANCE

Saturday date night was fun, with couples eventually separating into groups of male and female. The female chatter turned into gossip and continued into the late evening.

As I arrived at church the next morning, my heart was burdened with the words and stories spoken and heard. The habit of gossip had been with me for years, and I struggled to relinquish the hold it had on my tongue and relationships.

I sat alone in the car, burdened with guilt and remorse, and cried to God, "Please forgive me for falling back into the pit of gossip. I am sorry I sinned against You and the ones who were the topic of conversation."

With head and hands resting on the steering wheel, five words were gently spoken into my heart. "Go and sin no more." In scripture,[7] Jesus spoke these very words to a woman caught in sin. His forgiveness to this woman was immediate, and His command to her was to walk away from the sin, reclaim her life, and not allow the same sin to overtake her again. In His way, He was speaking into my tender heart that I was forgiven, and I was to move forward without the sin of gossip touching my lips again. When I found the story in scripture, I was humbled that He would minister to me so quickly with forgiveness and, at the same time, give me encouragement to continue my journey toward becoming more like Him.

FOLLOWING CHRIST

Write the Bible reference or quote from this chapter you would like to research.

Reflections: (Reflect on what resonates with you from this chapter.)

Focus Areas: (Where do you see areas to draw closer to God?)

Actions: (What will I do this week based on my focus areas?)

Prayer: (Pen a prayer to God, inviting Him into this area of your life.)

CHAPTER 9

STUMBLING BLOCKS AND STEPPING STONES

*"Let us throw off everything that hinders and the sin that
so easily entangles and let us run with perseverance the race
marked out for us. Let us fix our eyes on Jesus."* [1]

Reading scripture and practicing the presence of God opened my
eyes to spiritual things, and I began writing studies and stories to
share on the Dragonfly Ministries website. Putting words on paper
allowed me to process my thoughts and formulate them into words.
Writing was a healing process, as I realized I had a voice and could
use this new passion not only to express myself, but also to bring the
Bible to applicable teaching for those visiting the website.

But I needed local helpers with different skillsets to bring life to the
website and yellow paper vision. Who were God's chosen helpers

for this task? As I prayed, I saw three faces; two women I briefly met when I spoke at the women's conference, and Patty.[2] Patty was a dear friend, and I was excited God included her in the plan, but insecurities of pursuing these other two women rose higher than my fear of public speaking, teaching women the Bible, or developing a website.

FROM STUMBLING BLOCK TO STEPPING STONE

Each time God stretched me, I wanted to run and hide. But each time, He showed me how to overcome the stumbling block of fear and use it as a stepping stone to become stronger in Him. Transforming fear into a stepping stone, however, is not as simple as wishful thinking. Fear is an emotion hidden deep within the psyche, holding on with a grip that can be paralyzing and destructive. To step into obedience in the face of fear is to grab hold of courage, close the mind to any temptation of backing down, and ignorantly move forward to do what must be done. I say ignorantly because when fear is present, it is hard to rationally think of what lies ahead, of what the courageous movement will bring, or what doors may be opened. Fear often paralyzes discernment.

On the other hand, a stepping stone creates a pathway, holds weight, and provides a firm place to stand. Consider this: scripture says, "He set my feet on a rock and gave me a firm place to stand."[3] How God can take one courageous action of a fearful person and bring victory is beyond me. To overcome fear, face it. Then use it as a step to the next fear, which must also be overcome. With each step, fear is faced. It can be fear of being stretched, of learning a new skill, of rejection, or fear of failure. Each captured fear becomes a stepping stone into future and freedom.

The Pursuit of Ministry Partners

As God opened the door for Dragonfly Ministries, I began seeing the enemy's ambush set against me in childhood to keep me from building relationships with women. The fear of rejection had been a handicap for years, and I knew insecurities and fear either limit or catapult.

I wanted to conquer this fear and use it as a stepping stone on my journey into God's plan.

God gave me the inspiration to step into the battle of fear, and He encouraged me with direct instructions. My responsibility was to take the initiative; His was the results. I put on my big-girl pants[4] and stepped into the fear of pursuit.

The first woman on my short list was someone I had met at the conference.[5] After speaking, I was asked to lead a small discussion group. As I stepped into the room and made my way to an empty chair, my eyes locked gaze with a woman whose countenance reflected the peace of Christ. We didn't exchange contact information, nor did we take time to extend pleasantries. God's peace in her calmed me in my time of need. Now, God was placing her on my heart as a ministry partner. "Lord, I don't know her, I don't even know her name. She will think I'm nuts to invite her to be part of some new ministry named after an insect." God hounded me at every argument. This was His ministry, and she was His choice.

I contacted the church and spoke with the conference leader. After giving a description of the woman, she said the woman was named Martha,[6] and she would ask Martha to contact me. Martha did not contact me. After a week, I went to the church to see if I could get contact information. Though against their policy to share personal data, I did learn where Martha worked. I went to her workplace, and she "wasn't available to meet." Clearly, God was teaching me about pursuit. Her workplace did, however, give me her business card.

I called, left a message, and sent a short email; no response from either. Four failed attempts, and I was done. "Lord, she does not want to talk to me." My insecurities were screaming to forget it. After all, didn't my actions qualify as stalking? Yet, the Lord persisted. I sent another email using a lot of words to explain the dragonfly story, the Bible study for the affluent women, the website, and the call I sensed on her to be part of whatever this ministry was to become. History proves she finally called back and said yes. (Martha and I often laugh at the difficulty we had connecting. I do believe God held her back in responding so He could stretch me in learning to step out and pursue.)

The second was Jennifer,[7] the conference worship leader. After my speaking session, Jennifer talked with some women as I struggled with invisibility in the same room. Thoughts of failure plagued me. "You said too much." "You were too vulnerable." "Who do you think you are? These women are better Christians than you." "Nobody wants to talk to a freak like you." Unbeknownst to me, God had placed within Jennifer the words of comfort needed to soothe my raw heart. As if on cue, Jennifer left the crowded circle and approached me with words that blasted my invisibility cloak and brought me back to purpose. "You are an anointed and gifted speaker. God will give you many opportunities to share your story with others."

Jennifer was easier to locate, as her contact information was on her publicity materials. I connected with her through a series of hits and misses. She stood me up for the first lunch appointment (we showed up at different restaurants at the right time on the right date.) The next date, I went to her house, and she didn't open the door (she was blow drying her hair and didn't hear the doorbell). The verbiage in my head was sinister and sounded something like this: "She doesn't want to meet with you." "Her affirming words were only because she felt sorry for you." "She's avoiding you; don't you get it? Give up." But again, the Lord's prompting was louder than the verbiage in my head, so I stalked her, as had become my custom in the pursuit of women. We finally met, and by the end of the discussion, she was on board.

And so was Patty. Since we worked together and she had previously pursued me; since she had walked me through a kidney donation; and since she was key to my spiritual awakening, she was easier to invite into the ministry. She was the icing on the cake. And we were a team of four women, pursuing God's dream for a ministry.

"THE WAIT" | STILL WAITING

We met regularly to pray about Dragonfly Ministries. Our first order of business was in getting to know one another. Patty and I had done life together, but Martha, Jennifer, and Patty had never met; and as I stated earlier, I had only met Martha and Jennifer once before inviting them into ministry. Who were these women handpicked by God to be in ministry together? What did each bring to the table? How would God use each person's gifts and talents to bring His vision to life?

Our second order of business was in seeking God for His plan, laid out step by step. We had lots of questions with answers only God could provide. What was this ministry? What was the purpose and mission? Where was God leading? How were we to proceed? Who would write? What would we write about? How would the ministry be funded? Would we branch off into conferences or retreats? Was publishing in our future?

We had more questions than answers and knew our best step forward was to wait on God to reveal and open the way. We knew we were not to take a step until we were sure it was God's leading. From my past, I knew leading God was the complete opposite of being led by God and stirred up more messes than I cared to step into. In this instance, past mistakes proved to be a great marker for moving forward with God. He was the leader, and I would follow.

In the meantime, we did the last thing God directed. We built the website ministry with stories, devotionals, and testimonies. We met regularly to pray, and we celebrated God's faithfulness. As we waited, God worked in our hearts to prepare us for the call.

FOLLOWING CHRIST

Write the Bible reference or quote from this chapter you would like to research.

Reflections: (Reflect on what resonates with you from this chapter.)

Focus Areas: (Where do you see areas to draw closer to God?)

Actions: (What will I do this week based on my focus areas?)

Prayer: (Pen a prayer to God, inviting Him into this area of your life.)

CHAPTER 10

THE MINISTRY MANTLE

"Speak, Lord, for your servant is listening." [1]

RETREAT MINISTRY

As we prayed about the direction of Dragonfly Ministries, we sensed the call to usher others into the power of God's presence, free from distractions. We began praying about adding a retreat ministry. After two years, we hosted a retreat weekend in East Texas which provided attendees a five-hour block of quiet time to spend with God. We knew we were stepping into an uncomfortable zone for women, as most retreats allowed Saturday afternoon for shopping or crafting. We were also aware offering quiet time with God would keep our numbers low, as the sum of quiet plus God equals intimidation.

Our first retreat was themed "In the Stillness." We sent the attendees into their quiet time with these instructions: "Don't be afraid or anxious. If you are tired, take a nap with the awareness you are not alone. If you take a hike, do it with the awareness you are not alone. Invite the Holy Spirit into whatever you are doing or thinking. Talk and listen."

Five hours of quiet time was a bit intimidating for everyone, including me. What was I to do? What if I didn't hear from God during this quiet time? I was the leader, and if He didn't speak to me, how would that look?[2]

For the first two hours, I pressured the Holy Spirit, "Speak to me, speak to me." No word, no prompting, no scripture, not a whisper. I lay on a blanket in the warm Texas sun and took a nap. When I awakened, I went for a walk, rushing the Holy Spirit to speak to me. I wanted to scream at Him, "Don't make me look bad! I'm doing what You asked, and You're hiding." I was fearful I would be the only person who did not experience the presence of God in her quiet time.

Four hours and forty-five minutes into the silence, I walked to the lake and sat with my feet in the water, wondering why God was silent. A dragonfly landed and lingered on the lily pad by my feet. I smiled. God used our love language, the dragonfly, to remind me of our history together and His faithfulness, even when I could not hear or sense Him.

After quiet time, women shared how God had met them through a song, nature, scripture, a picture or a memory. We witnessed God's healing presence as women shared hurts, unforgiveness, and fears.

**Quiet time produced change, for to come into
His presence is to be forever changed.**

We pressed forward with retreat ministry for ten years in various states. We witnessed God's power in miracles of healing and deliverance. God added community, leaders, and prayer warriors to our circle of dragonflies. He developed leadership that would touch communities post-retreat. Never underestimate what God can do in a block of time if you allow Him to speak into your heart.

STORIES OF CHANGE | PRAY FOR ME

One Saturday evening, we closed our final session and invited those wanting prayer to hang around. The room was filled with excitement and laughter as I noticed a young woman motioning me to come near. I approached and knelt in front of her. She whispered, "Pray for me." Oh, the beauty of a humble heart admitting the need for prayer.

I wanted to take her in my arms and hold her. But rather, I lifted her into the arms of God through prayer. As we prayed, the noise in the background faded. At the close of my prayer, another woman began to pray, and then another. This un-orchestrated prayer happened in God's beautiful way, and His presence rained down as we saw peace and calm pour into the one who had lifted those three words, "Pray for me."

STORIES OF CHANGE | THE LIST

Various women had shared testimonies and stories. The Saturday night session was coming to an end when I saw a raised hand in the back of the meeting room.

The hand raiser was one who seldom spoke. Her story went something like this:

"I knew there would be quiet time, so I made a list of everything I wanted to talk to God about. I pulled out my list, but the Holy Spirit stopped me. He had a list to work through first. I was in disbelief. You have a list for me?

His list had one word. Forgiveness. He told me I needed to forgive the one who had abused me in my youth. My entire quiet time was spent on this one list item. I didn't understand why He would want me to do such a thing. I didn't ask for the abuse, I wanted to forget it, and I didn't want to share it with anyone.

But He convinced me forgiveness was for my healing and my journey. Forgiveness would release me to grow in Him and allow me to move forward. As I sat with God, He gave me the grace to say the words, "I forgive the one who hurt me." I know forgiveness will be a process because I've held this hurt for many years. But I know God will walk me through this until complete forgiveness comes."

STORIES OF CHANGE | PSALM 139

Many retreats were attended by women who were afraid to step into quiet time because they were unfamiliar with God and His ways. One such woman did not own a Bible, nor did she know how to go about being with God. We opened her Bible to Psalm 139 and instructed her to spend her quiet time reading the entire chapter. I instructed her, when you come to a verse that resonates with your spirit, stop. Read it again. Write the verse in your journal, and then write down the thoughts or questions that come to mind from that verse. Why is it important to you? What questions arise when you read it? What do you think God is saying to you personally? Write a letter to God, expressing your thoughts. When she came out of her quiet time, she had a beautiful story to share. She hadn't gotten past the first verse, "O Lord, You have searched me and You know me."[3] Her story was something like this. "While growing up, I was the middle child and got lost in the mix. After reading this verse, I spent my entire time talking to God about who I am and all the feelings that surfaced because He knows me."

STORIES OF CHANGE | A CHANGED ATTITUDE

When my friend Marian attended a Dragonfly Ministries retreat weekend, she brought baggage containing anger toward God that she had not been willing to work through. As a matter of fact, she told me she wasn't interested in talking to Him at all. After arriving at the retreat location, it occurred to Marian she was going to spend time alone with God. I said, "Let me get this straight. You're angry with God, you haven't talked to Him about your situation, and you don't want to talk to Him about it. And yet you are at a Dragonfly retreat where you know you are going to have some quiet time to spend with God?" We laughed together, and by the time her quiet time was over, there was a restored peace in Marian's life. She was back on speaking terms with God. From that quiet time, she came to know God as the One who forgives and restores.

THE MINISTRY MANTLE

The role of Dragonfly Ministries was defined. We were to be God's dragonflies, pulling in His love and grace, reflecting Christ to the world. We were to walk so closely with Him that His character would become our character, our hearts would reflect His heart, and our life journey would cause others to want more of Him. This would require being emptied of wrong teaching, religious thinking, self-centered living, and striving for man's approval.

It would also require an understanding of "the wait" and the importance of allowing God to work *through* us rather than us working *for* God. When God works *through* His vessel, He directs the path and goes ahead to clear the way. He does the work, directs the work, and is responsible for the results of the work. He carries the burden. When we work *for* God, we tell Him which direction we are taking, invite Him to follow us, ask him to bless the work, and we take responsibility for the results. This is the heavy yoke.

As leader of Dragonfly Ministries, I carried the mantle[4] (or responsibility and authority) for this ministry. In His grace, I stepped into the divine assignment, confident God would remove all boulders so I could scale the ministry mountain in record time. He prepared me with a kidney donation, the gift of hearing His voice, a ministry and website, and ministry partners. I was ready to take on the world.

But behind the scenes, danger lurked. With each step into obedience, the aftershocks caught me off guard and threatened to throw me off course. Rubble and stumbling blocks were scattered everywhere, and advancement into ministry would be put on hold. Seeds of pride and a desire to be adored were hidden motives not yet revealed. I walked in darkness, doing ministry from a heart that desired to please God, yet operating out of seeking admiration. The need for man's approval needed to be uprooted before God would move me into the full realm of His plan. Uprooting an established plant takes time, shakes the foundation, and upsets everything around it. A great shaking was coming, and, by the grace of God, I was oblivious to what lay ahead. The question, "Do you trust Me?" was to be asked many times in the shaking. Obedience is not for weenies.

FOLLOWING CHRIST

Write the Bible reference or quote from this chapter you would like to research.

Reflections: (Reflect on what resonates with you from this chapter.)

Focus Areas: (Where do you see areas to draw closer to God?)

Actions: (What will I do this week based on my focus areas?)

Prayer: (Pen a prayer to God, inviting Him into this area of your life.)

CHAPTER 11

A HOME CALLED SANCTUARY

"God is our refuge and strength, an ever-present help in trouble." [1]

THE WINDS OF CHANGE

As Dragonfly Ministries celebrated its third anniversary, I sensed the winds of change. At first it was a gentle breeze blowing to prepare us for transition.[2] I leaned into the Lord and asked, "What is this coming change?"

I had only perceived the winds of change one other time. When we lived in North Carolina, I sensed God was in the process of relocating us. I didn't know where, but I knew it would be my role to encourage forever husband to leave the east coast and take whatever career opportunities lay ahead. Shortly afterwards, his employer invited us to relocate to Texas, which had been a fruitful endeavor.

But now, this same sense of change was stirring up great uncertainty. Our daughters were married with established Texas roots, and our first grandchild was due. Texas was the holder of my heart, family, friends, ministry, and identity. How could I be expected to relocate?

And there it was again, the question from God, "Do you trust Me?" Clearly, if I did, He would not be asking this yet again. I had no immediate answer. Could I trust Him with my family, the expense of relocating, caring for the daughters and their families, the sons in a new community and school, and the ministry? Could He possibly work all things together[3] so they made sense?

It was as if I were holding a box of puzzle pieces, each piece from a different puzzle, being asked to take two pieces and put them together when none of the pieces seemed to fit.

I thought back to the move to Texas and how God orchestrated the relocation to give Johnston's mom a kidney. I recollected how we were quickly established in the neighborhood with friends and ministry. I recalled how God directed me in the pursuit of Martha and Jennifer and how He blessed those friendships immensely. After looking back at God's provision in Texas, I could respond, "Yes, Lord, I trust You."

Shortly after sensing the winds of change, forever husband's employer invited us to relocate to Baltimore, Maryland. We sold our home in Texas, found the home of our dreams in Maryland, said good-bye to family and friends, and set out on a great adventure. (Oh, if only it were that carefree and simple!)

A HOME CALLED SANCTUARY

We seemed to move at the height of winter. Our move to Texas had been in January, and our moving truck had been delayed by two days due to an ice storm. Now we were in Maryland, amid a snowstorm and 12-degree weather, again waiting on the arrival of a moving truck. Excitement was in the air as I looked forward to what God had in store. Nervous anticipation was in the minds of the sons who would start school mid-year, and eagerness to get settled into his new work was forever husband's immediate priority. Welcome to Maryland.

Our new home was situated on an acre of land, replenished with wildflower gardens, a gazebo, an in-ground swimming pool, and a deck across the back of the house. Heavily treed woods provided privacy around 2/3 of the house. It was peaceful, spacious, and a place for family, friends and ministry. But the relocation to Maryland was not without tears or grief.

Within the first week of arriving, I received word my father had passed.[4] I had visited him two weeks prior, knowing he was on his way out of this life. I loved and adored Dad and knew he loved me unconditionally. He accepted me no matter what mistakes I made. To be with him was to be home. He had been through cancer treatments twice, and God extended his years, I'm sure, because of prayers from his four children.

But in this new land, I was alone with pain and grief as I unpacked our belongings. I had grieved my father's disease of cancer and emphysema, knowing one would eventually take his life. Now was a season to grieve his passing. In addition to grieving the loss of dad and other familiarities of life, my heart longed for our daughters. I asked,

"Lord, why must we be separated from the daughters and their families?"

His response,

"My child, you have the peace of knowing your children will be with you throughout eternity. I have brought you here to bring many of My children to Me. As you entrust the care of your daughters into My hands, I entrust the care of My children into your hands.[5] Be faithful with the ones I bring you as I am faithful with the ones you have entrusted to Me."

SUFFICIENT GRACE

One evening, in the throes of grief, I drew a hot bath, so I could drown my sorrow.[6] As I soaked, I man-cried. Heavy guttural sounds were forced from my depth as I mourned. As the tears fell and met the steam rising from the water, they seemed to burst into hopelessness and fear. I was alone. Where was I to turn for comfort? How would we be able to hit the ground running in this new land surrounded by such sadness?

The Lord tenderly spoke four words, "My grace is sufficient."[7] In the following days as grief presented, I rehearsed those four words as a reminder my Heavenly Father was with me, loved me unconditionally, accepted me regardless of life choices, and would give me the strength to continue forward.

Forever husband responded to my grief and loneliness in practical ways. He suggested I come with him to work on a part-time basis to help him through his marketing season. He also began the search for a church home, knowing connection with a church family would be a surefire way to develop friendships.

SETTLING IN

We joined our "new" church home within a month of arriving and were quickly absorbed in church ministry and relationships. Forever husband came into Maryland with a spiritual desire to learn, grow, and serve. This move fueled his desire to know God more fully. He initiated our involvement with an evangelistic outreach ministry commenting, "I know God brought us here for a purpose and we don't need to waste any time." It was as if God put him on a fast track to spiritual growth and forever husband was moving quickly. With two hearts opened to spiritual things, we could talk about God's presence, goodness, and inner workings in our lives. The strength and depth of our relationship began picking up steam.

I stepped into the volunteer role of Women's Ministry Director for the church,[8] where I embraced the opportunity to initiate and develop friendships with women. God brought me full circle from fear of rejection to initiating friendships. Through this ministry and these women, He also began expanding my leadership skills.

As a united front, forever husband and I opened our home for mini-retreats and women's ministry events. The swimming pool was used by church families for bar-b-ques and parties. We welcomed out of town visitors and family members for extended stays. Forever husband and I spent many weekends floating in the pool, ankles locked together so we would not drift apart. Everything about the home was peaceful. It was as though God surrounded the property with guardian angels and gave us a home called "sanctuary"[9] to grow and prepare us for days ahead.

CHANGING FAMILY DYNAMICS

These were also years of changing family dynamics; forever husband and I were stretched to parent teenage sons on the heels of hair rebellion,[10] in the throes of puberty, overthrowing our taste in music to discover their own,[11] and reaching for freedom from the grip of parental control.

Parenting young children has its challenges but also comes with the blessing of knowing we control bedtime, mealtime, playdates, haircuts, clothing, the radio and television stations, and time spent on gaming. As children grow into teens, parental control becomes "perceived control" as teens find ways to meet their own "needs." For instance, teens have an interesting way of swapping clothes with friends, acquiring cigarettes, hanging with questionable companions, skipping classes, etc. They make their own way. It's been happening for years and will not be shut down because a parent is frustrated or makes demands. It's just the way of the teenage world and their quest for independence.

We navigated this unknown territory as best we could, but I could see the toll on all three alpha males living in the home. Arguments over hair styles, homework, chores, and friends were commonplace, and the sons started pulling away from forever husband because they felt his demands were archaic and restrictive. I tried to stay out of the mix, but it was harder than I realized to allow division to come into a family once unified. Forever husband's control stepped in, and I wanted to step away, but responsibility of a parent doesn't end when children become challenging. I was called to honor forever husband, raise the sons in a godly manner, and follow Jesus, whatever the cost. Times were confusing and hard, but still, in God's special way, the home provided a sanctuary of peace and rest.

MINISTRY UPDATE

While in Maryland, Dragonfly Ministries published a children's book,[12] the website continued to gain traffic, and we added more retreats to meet the demands of attendees wanting their family and friends to experience the power of God at a retreat weekend. The retreat ministry brought lasting life change to hundreds of women as they experienced intimacy with Christ during their quiet time. God raised leaders in every state where retreats were hosted. He provided finances, worship leaders, facilities, and attendees.

By God's grace, despite my hesitancy, we experienced ministry growth. From the beginning of Dragonfly Ministries, I fought the leadership role. "Lord, bring someone else to lead this ministry. Surely, You've made a mistake. You can't mean me." But God persisted. The vision drawn on the yellow legal pad with a number 2 lead pencil was given to me and I was the one called to carry the ministry forward. In His time. In His way. He would lead and I would follow; and when I got the order of this directive wrong, weakness and sin would both be exposed.

After a short while, I reverted to self-dependence and started to feel the burden of responsibility for growing the ministry "in His time and in His way." People expected it to grow more quickly and look different. Some wanted to rework our mission statement and leadership style. Others expressed complaint and criticism over small details. Each expression of dissatisfaction burdened my heart. I felt personally attacked because I took ownership of something that belonged to God. I was in God's school of leadership, and He used the very people I was leading to teach the good, the bad, the lonely, the blessings, and the ugly of ministry. He also used them to expose areas of weakness in my limited leadership skills.

The biggest weakness was the desire to please everyone. There were situations where I would disappoint women because I did not meet their expectations, or I would not bow to their needs. There were other times when I would bow to their needs and then be disciplined by God, because this was His ministry and He made the decisions, not women who wanted a part of His ministry. I strived to grow the ministry, to take the suggestions made by others and roll them into the vision. But every attempt hit a brick wall. So, I tried harder. Better advertisements, bigger mailing lists, silent auctions to raise funds. The voices became louder than the voice of God and striving to please people brought bitterness of heart. The harder I strived, the more burdensome it became. I had taken full responsibility for a retreat ministry I was never intended to carry. I lost passion for ministry. All ministry.

I heard a voice say, "Step aside from the retreat ministry. Others will lead. I have not called you to this. I have called you to teach and write. You are carrying what has not been given to you." But I could not step aside. This was my identity—in Texas and in Maryland. The adoration of the attendees had become my self-worth. Friends told me retreats would not be the same without me. When I tried to back out, I was met with disappointment. It seemed the retreats were taking on a double billing—Mary and God. Which were people really coming to see? It was time for me to step aside, but I could not bring myself to disappoint. I justified involvement by questioning whether the voice to "step aside" had been from God or the enemy.

I didn't realize the depth of bitterness or pain taking root in my heart by my need to be admired, nor did I understand the lesson of following God even when His direction went against the counsel of man. His school of leadership training had begun. The ongoing chapter was titled, "Trusting God. His time. His way."

THE WINDS OF CHANGE RETURN

Our Maryland home was a land of rest and retreat. Our family years in Maryland were short but powerful as God began positioning our family on the rock of Christ as we worshipped, served, and prayed together.

Forever husband was steeped into his job and working 16-hour days. As I was finding my identity in the children, Dragonfly Ministries, and serving the women of the church, he found his in the job. He was a great provider for our family and his employer was grateful for his work ethic and business success.

After three years in Maryland, the winds of change again began to blow. Forever husband indicated there was no discussion of a possible sale or relocation of the company, but the Lord continued to impress on my heart, "Keep your head down, get the house and gardens ready for sale. You will be leaving soon." So, I prepared for the inevitable. We would relocate again. But where? At this point, it didn't matter. I knew, no matter where He sent us, my answer would always be, "Yes, Lord."

BOOKENDS OF GRIEF

I entered Maryland grieving the death of my father. God's grace carried us thus far, but as we prepared to leave Maryland, a new grief swept over me—not only the grief of leaving a land fruitful and fulfilling, but a grief that our new land would carry a heaviness and sadness I was unsure God's grace could cover. It was as if this chapter of our lives had been held in place with bookends of grief.

I dreaded the days ahead. I did not look forward to the new land as I had looked forward to Maryland. Though I knew God had prepared us and was sending us forth, I also knew there would be enemies and ambushes set against us. I feared our family was not ready or strong enough to head into this battleground. Our family foundation in Christ had a three-year lifespan; we were still babies, not ready to do battle.

One evening as I journaled, I was sure God spoke these words of preparation to me:

> "The next season will be a very difficult one. The power of My presence in and around you will shake and reposition your foundation. Do not fear. I am moving things in the spiritual realm but I have prepared an army to help. Go and possess the land. Do not be afraid."

But I was afraid. Very afraid. We were headed into a storm. Would our anchor hold us steady, or would the tossing of the waves tear us apart? He had prepared me, as always. But this time, it was not for a home called "sanctuary"; it was for a land called "desolate."

> Lord, go before us and prepare the way. Have mercy on us, O Lord, Amen.

FOLLOWING CHRIST

Write the Bible reference or quote from this chapter you would like to research.

Reflections: (Reflect on what resonates with you from this chapter.)

Focus Areas: (Where do you see areas to draw closer to God?)

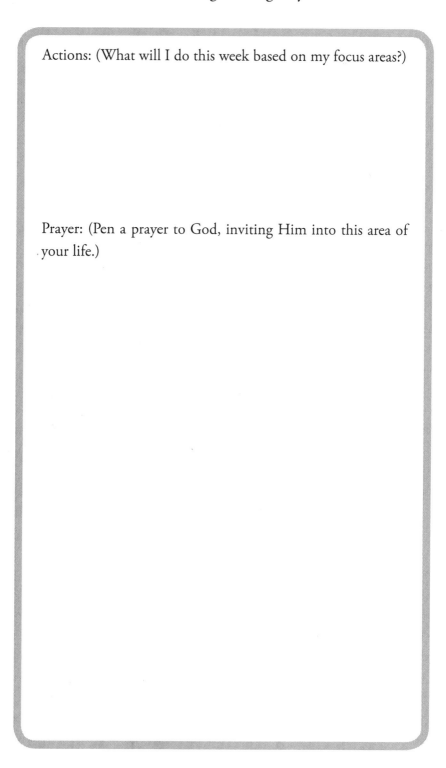

Actions: (What will I do this week based on my focus areas?)

Prayer: (Pen a prayer to God, inviting Him into this area of your life.)

CHAPTER 12

CHICAGOLAND

"For our light and momentary troubles are achieving for us
an eternal glory that far outweighs them all, so we fix our eyes
not on what is seen. For what is seen is temporary, but what
is unseen is eternal." [1]

CHICAGOLAND

We left Maryland in late November, ahead of the moving truck
and a winter storm. Forever husband and one son traveled in the
van. The other son rode with me as I drove the car. The sons were
uncommunicative on the journey from Maryland to Illinois, upset
at the relocation and disruption of life. We had been in Maryland
a little over three years, and it had taken that long for them to feel
established. Now the rug was pulled from under them again, and
they were in solemn limbo. The thought of starting over in a new

place sickened and angered them. The drive was long, quiet, and discouraging. We arrived amid the first snowfall of the season. Welcome to Chicagoland.

We also arrived without passion or zeal for the days ahead. Moving from place to place had taken its toll on our family and was proving to be more stressful than we had imagined. Forever husband buried himself in his work. My heart ached for sons who dreaded the navigation of the unfamiliar and the lack of community around them. As for me, I wanted to be back in Texas near the daughters' families, the grandchildren, ministry, and friends. Deep loneliness returned and set up shop as I moved through the rote of all that comes with moving.

I thought back to an acquaintance who had "put her foot down"[2] with her husband about relocating. She told him she would not move for his career, and if he was ever offered a promotion or transfer involving relocation, he could go without her or find another job.

Perhaps I should have taken that posture when we started out in the Carolinas. But as I spoke my marriage vows, my stance was to love, honor, and support forever husband, which included his career. My role as wife was to go wherever he went, embrace the new land and people, and see how God might orchestrate each move to enrich our lives.[3] In loving, honoring and supporting forever husband, I honored God.[4]

But grief also accompanied me in this move. Just as we moved the sons from state to state, we had also moved the daughters in a similar way. Stability of a homestead was not one of the blessings of their lives, rather disruption had become their norm. The daughters had since settled in north Texas with husbands and were starting their families; they survived the chaos of relocation. My prayer for the sons was the same, in that the moves would make them stronger rather than bitter or resentful. "The Lord bless you and keep you"[5] became my parting prayer for them as they left the house each morning to board the school bus. Lonely days ensued as we each tried to find our place in the new land.

THE CHURCH SEARCH

Because we had been so enmeshed in our Maryland church, we quickly set out to find a church home in Illinois. We understood the importance of getting teenagers involved in a church where they would be accepted, meet friends, and find a place to belong. We decided we would know our "new church home" by the reception the sons received when we walked into the church.

One Sunday we visited a small church, hidden from the road by a line of trees. As we walked into the vestibule, the youth pastor made a beeline to meet the sons. We attended the church service as a family and lingered afterwards to speak with the pastor. When it was time to leave, we could not locate the sons. A search of the building produced no results.

After a few minutes, three boys appeared. At first sight, they looked the same. Same hairstyle, skinny jeans, band t-shirts, and all three were smiling. Who was this boy who could easily pass for a brother? His name was Andy. Where had they been? Hanging out in the Pastor's office. What were they doing in the pastor's office? Andy was the pastor's son, and he was hosting a church tour for Tyler and Patrick.

The icing on the cake? Andy lived in our neighborhood. He was instrumental in introducing the sons to kids in the neighborhood and at school. What sweetness we found in the answered prayer as

God brought such a perfect match into our lives. Andy had the same interests in hairstyles, music, gaming, bands, and skateboarding. God directed us not only to our church home but also to a best friend for the sons.

God heard my prayer for friendship. This time, the prayer was lifted for the sons. God provided a friend both sons could enjoy and who would be key in helping them get settled.

THE CHURCH WALLS EXTENDED

The church was also catalyst in staving off my loneliness. After one church service, Jamie approached me, introduced herself, and proceeded with, "I am looking for someone to lead a Bible study for a group of friends who don't know Jesus. Would you be willing to open your home and lead us?"

My spoken answer was "yes." My unspoken thoughts were more in the line of "Why me? You don't even know me." We exchanged contact information. I shook my head in disbelief of God's orchestration of whatever that was, and we left the building. Over the course of a few months, our ladies gathering grew into a group of twelve. We met weekly for a devotional, Bible discussion, and dinner. The group consisted of believers, non-believers, and seekers. It was a safe place for those hungry for community and God's truth.

TEACH ME THE BIBLE

I posted invitations to our gatherings in various coffee shops and received a phone call from Carol. She was not interested in joining our study, she didn't know much about the Bible, and she had a few questions about Christianity. Could I meet with her one on one?

When I met Carol, her first words made me smile. "Mary, I just have a few questions about the Bible and being a Christian, and I wonder if you will help me. But you need to know, I am not a Christian and it's not your job to save me."[6] I gave a dramatic sigh of relief and said, "I could not save you if I wanted to. But I am glad to answer any questions I can, and I'm glad to help you navigate the Bible."

Carol and I started reading the Bible; yes, we started in Genesis, and yes, I recommended a study Bible for her to purchase. When our reading advanced to the book of I Kings, Carol stated, "Mary, my spirit is dry, I am thirsty. Do you think we can move to the New Testament so I can learn about Jesus?" Just days later, as we met to discuss our New Testament reading, she reached across the table, placed her hand on mine, and said, "Mary, I'm a Christian now."

God again provided a safe place for someone to read through scripture, and He did the work of salvation. My role was simply to be obedient and journey with Carol through scripture.

There were many similarities in Illinois reminding me of God's provision in Texas. As God used Patty in Texas to invite me into a study with a group of women, He used Jamie to do the same in Illinois. As God used a neighborhood boy in Texas to answer my prayers, He used a neighborhood boy in Illinois as an answered prayer for the sons. And as God invited me into His work to bring salvation to the affluent woman and her friends, He also invited me to be a part of Carol's salvation. There was no doubt God had us in Illinois for a purpose.

FOLLOWING CHRIST

Write the Bible reference or quote from this chapter you would like to research.

Reflections: (Reflect on what resonates with you from this chapter.)

Focus Areas: (Where do you see areas to draw closer to God?)

Actions: (What will I do this week based on my focus areas?)

Prayer: (Pen a prayer to God, inviting Him into this area of your life.)

CHAPTER 13

THE LAND CALLED DESOLATE

"Stand at the crossroads and look; ask for the ancient paths,
ask where the good way is, and walk in it, and you will find
rest for your souls." [1]

Lord, Your child is afraid.

"Be strong and courageous; this is the path I have chosen for you." [2]

Yes, Lord.

CLIMATE SHIFTS AND SPIRITUAL STORMS

As we worked to make Chicagoland our home and embrace the new adventure, my spiritual guard was down. I was not looking for what was wrong, but what was right. The climate shifted, and we found ourselves amid a great storm—not a snowstorm, but a spiritual storm that seemed to happen overnight without warning. Beneath the surface of our family foundation lay a rumbling that would eventually bring an earthquake of division and produce a tsunami that would overpower any storm I feared.

Forever husband was struggling. His work was not as demanding as previous jobs. He had time to himself, and he began questioning his identity. As he inventoried his life, he found he was not satisfied with where he was or who he was married to. Everything fell under a microscope, and I became the magnified target of his discontent and anger, which produced an uprising of pride in him and despair in me.

Pride is destructive. It says, "Don't tell me what to do or how to do it."

Pride says, "My way is best, no matter what you say." It says, "Don't allow anyone else to be right. If attacked, take defense and create drama and strife." It seemed forever husband was bent on breaking me down so his pride would be lifted. His will against mine was not a pretty combination, and I did my best to fall into the shadows and allow him to "win" as much as possible. My voice was becoming diminished, as was my confidence and feeling of significance.

Who was this man? He had always been an opinioned, headstrong, outspoken, and passionate man but we were a great match in that way, as I needed someone I could not bowl over with stubbornness, and he needed someone to bring gentleness to his strength. But now, he was not interested in my opinion nor gentleness and winning arguments was more important than building our relationship. The air carried an oppressive heaviness, depression settled into my heart, and darkness was closing in.

Though forever husband was physically present in the house, he was not engaged with the family. His emotional withdrawal signaled red flags, and my insecurities flared as I fought to be seen, heard, and loved. His anger flared as he demanded respect and privacy. Arguments ensued, and a cycle of resentment, bitterness, and criticism swirled like gale force winds. The disagreements fueled the winds, and they became stronger and stronger. We had gone from a home called "sanctuary" to a land called "desolate," and we were entering the eye of the storm.

LOSE YOUR VOICE

Because of my lack of emotional maturity and confidence, I struggled with issues and questions I had no power to control. What could I do to fix the problem? Where had I failed him? Had I not moved from land to land in support of his career? Had God not put us together to change the world for Christ? Where was my value? Who was I apart from being his wife? Did I even matter? How could it be I was to blame for everything in his life that had gone sour? Was I truly a bad wife and a terrible mom? How could he "love me but not be in love with me"? Was it true I could not do anything to make him happy and I had managed to say or do something that was a marriage deal breaker?

I tried to appease forever husband, to meet his demands to be a perfect wife. But regardless of what I did, he found fault. My character and spirituality were under attack. Why was I the target of his anger? When had I become the problem for his woes? What had I done to deserve the verbal attacks that never relinquished? These questions inhabited my thoughts as I tried to figure out steps to appease his anger.

In the middle of one argument, I inquired of the Holy Spirit how to respond to the accusations. I heard Him speak three words, "Lose your voice." What? Lose my voice? Are You sure? That meant no more taking offense or defense. No more desperate attempts to make him love me. I sensed God instructing me to humble myself by letting go of my "need" to be right. I did not savor the opportunity to lose an argument or be unjustly accused.

Out of obedience, I quieted my voice but was still filled with criticism, disappointment, and fear. My thoughts reflected my heart. "Out of the overflow of the heart the mouth speaks."[3]

When had I given way to allow such ugliness to enter? I needed a new heart, one filled with love and endurance, not one filled with pride and selfishness. Though I could not control the words spoken by forever husband, I could control my words and speak only when I could be encouraging and supportive. "Lord, change me."[4] I felt if I further opened my heart to God and allowed Him to change whatever it was forever husband didn't like about me, the marriage would be saved.

As I had done with Dragonfly Ministries, I was now doing with this marriage. I was holding the responsibility of something that was not mine to carry, and my desire to make forever husband happy drained my will to live and elevated my fear of rejection. Hopelessness and depression set in, as did the darkness of night.

A CONVERSATION WITH GOD

"In the midst of darkness, there is light. In the midst of light, there is sound. In the midst of sound, we find His voice. The power of His voice chops down the forest of confusion around us. The power of His voice creates a path in our wilderness. The power of His voice breaks the waters open and raises our heads above the waves of doubt, grief and despair towering around us. The power of His voice overcomes any strategy the enemy has developed to hold us captive in his chains of defeat."[5]

At some point in my journey, God taught me to hear His voice through journaling. As I would write prayers to Him, I would scribe the words flowing into my mind, as if I were transcribing a recording, comforted by the words being spoken. In looking back over conversations journaled during the years of darkness, I am comforted and reminded God sees our lives from the beginning to the end. He knows how our obedience will guard our life and destiny, and He truly directs us every step of the way. Below is one prayer that encouraged my heart:

My forever child,[6]

I know the desires of your heart, your aches and pain, your loneliness and longings. I sense your frustration and hurt. Don't linger in allowing Me to do the work I desire to do. Hold fast and steady to Me. Don't question My means, My ways, but trust wholly in Me, going as I direct without faltering or seeking man's counsel. Wait upon Me, not looking to the right or to the left. Walk behind Me all the way, allowing Me to lead. Step by step. Allow Me to relieve your frustrations and carry you safely. Though the waters rise, they will not overtake you. Though the storms rage, you are safe. I watch over you, protect and guard you, physically and spiritually.

I will not forsake your family, and I will not leave you.[7]

FOLLOWING CHRIST

Write the Bible reference or quote from this chapter you would like to research.

Reflections: (Reflect on what resonates with you from this chapter.)

Focus Areas: (Where do you see areas to draw closer to God?)

Actions: (What will I do this week based on my focus areas?)

Prayer: (Pen a prayer to God, inviting Him into this area of your life.)

CHAPTER 14

THE JOURNEY CALLED MIDLIFE

"See, I am sending an angel ahead of you to guard you along the way and to bring you to the place I have prepared." [1]

THE LIGHTHOUSE

My self-confidence was at an all-time low. My voice was silenced to avoid further breaking. The shell of Mary was dull, and the light within was snuffed out. In His kindness and at the peak of the brokenness and family destruction, God sent me back to work. Amid my storm, God tied my lifeboat to a lighthouse, a safe place—a church.

I inquired of the Lord why He had chosen this time, job description, and place. He responded, "I am sending you back to work for seven years.[2] In this role, you are My vessel for bringing unity to staff and shifting the culture. You are to water from underneath. As water feeds the roots under the soil, you are to refresh the staff through encouragement and prayer. Speak only as I direct, keep your head down, and meet every challenge. Pray for those you serve."

I was satisfied to be in a place where I could be quiet and get lost in the work; it was a great distraction and hiding place from the wreckage at home. I was content to be invisible. It was as though I was in an oaken barrel, tightly corked, fermenting in the fragrance of God's presence without emitting His aroma. I knew eventually He would open the way for me to share stories of His faithfulness through the kidney donation, the dragonfly sightings, etc. but for now, He provided a hiding place from the raging storm.

I tried to keep my personal life separate from work. I didn't want to be treated differently because of the personal storm, and I didn't want to dishonor forever husband by sharing his journey.[3] Perhaps he might step back into the church, and I didn't want anyone thinking poorly of him. Love always protects.[4] I determined to walk out the work journey the same way as my personal journey by leaning into God and bringing my "A" game to work, regardless of the challenges at home.

GOD'S DIVINE APPOINTMENT

While forever husband was rewriting history, speaking of our past years as though they had been a mistake, I was falling apart. My significance was entrenched in being his forever wife. I held the struggles closely, as I did not want others to think poorly of forever husband. I knew he was wrestling with something, but I did not know the root, nor did I want to dishonor him. God brought us to this place, and God would bring us through.

Out of desperation and in search of godly counsel, I met with a Christian counselor. I explained the verbal aggressiveness of forever husband and the crushing of my spirit. The immediate advice was, "file for divorce." I was dumbfounded. My stance was the complete opposite. I needed someone to help me understand what forever husband was struggling with, someone to pray with. His recent behavior was not typical of his personality; this was not the character of the man I had been married to for twenty-five years. Divorce was not in my vocabulary, and I would not entertain the thought of going down that road.

Still seeking wisdom, I met with another Christian counselor who stated I was overdramatizing and questioned me to figure out what I was doing wrong to cause forever husband to be angry. He labeled my concerns as "malarkey." Hope vanished. I could not find support in the professional Christian community to help make sense of the sudden change in forever husband's demeanor or character.

It was then I determined to walk this journey with God as my counselor and guide; to invite voices into this situation speaking from their soul, rather than as directed by the Holy Spirit, would be my downfall.

I had a trained spirit to hear God's voice and recognize His promptings. He had prepared me for this storm.

Whatever problems were present, I was to bring them to Him. Whatever setbacks presented themselves, He was to be my coach. I was to withhold the intimate details of this journey from bystanders to protect forever husband and to learn directly from God how to walk through it.

I was also aware God could bring a mentor into my life at any time, and I was to be open yet discerning in the relationships He put in front of me. And just like that, as the marital foundation was crumbling, God brought Laurie. When I first met her, we exchanged smiles as though we had known one another for years. And then a friendship began to blossom. Little did I know, God had appointed her to become my counselor and friend through the hardest season of life.

Laurie listened intently to my heartbreak, prayed with me, and immediately suspected what was taking place. She had walked a friend through a similar storm so she knew how to help me navigate this unfamiliar territory. She informed me forever husband was displaying the actions and attitudes of a man in midlife crisis and explained a lot of men go through this process and repeat the same lines to their wives. It's the way we know when a spouse is going through midlife—they go by an unrehearsed and unknown script. I found an article online that helped me further understand[5]:

THE HALLMARKS OF MIDLIFE CRISIS

"There are certain hallmarks of the midlife crisis that will always remain, so others who have walked the road before can recognize the condition and help the left behind spouse who is looking for guidance. The hallmarks are:

1. The emotional bomb drop that marks the start of the journey for the left-behind spouse but not the spouse in the midlife crisis;

2. The various ways of saying "I love you but I'm not in love with you," evidencing deep confusion about their feelings that had been so clear before;

3. The total withdrawing from the left-behind spouse;

4. The clear running behaviors that can include, but are not limited to, the midlife crisis affair;

5. The clear rebellion that is observed within the midlife spouse against everything they ever believed in, including the left-behind spouse, not to mention a great deal of spewing, confusion, and rewriting of history that deeply confuses the left-behind spouse. The left-behind spouse knows what they are hearing is not correct."

THE SIX STAGES OF A MIDLIFE CRISIS

In his book, *Men in Midlife*,[6] Jim Conway states this process can take anywhere from two to seven years; longer if a man refuses to address the issues. He further broke midlife crisis into six stages:

1.   Denial

2.   Anger

3.   Replay

4.   Depression

5.   Withdrawal

6.   Acceptance

I am not stating forever husband was going through midlife crisis, but I am saying he was a poster child for what I was learning, as if following a script. Character traits were showing up in the hallmarks of midlife crisis in different ways. I had seen glimpses of forever husband's anger through the past years of marriage, but they were short-lived, and he was apologetic afterwards. Now he was moving into full anger, and I didn't know how to navigate or help him, except to fight back or keep quiet. I chose to keep quiet and allow him to rule. There was no winning an argument against this man. He was gifted in arguing, he would not back down even if proven wrong, and he was well versed in escalating.

I am not an expert on midlife crisis, but I found two websites[7] that helped me understand the process and the decision-making taking place in these troubled years. When many adults reach a certain age, they pause to evaluate their lives; where they are, have been, and are headed. Some call this midlife. Some adults make a few tweaks and adjustments in their career, hobbies, spending, etc., and continue to move forward more fulfilled. Others come to a decision that their life needs a major overhaul and decisions are made in private, without the consultation of the spouse, which brings about a crisis. Crisis is defined as "an emotionally significant event or radical change of status in a person's life."[8]

No matter the prognosis, we were in crisis. Though I tried to put into practice what I was reading, it was too late. My spirit was crushed, my insecurities flared, and forever husband was now deep into emotional withdrawal, questioning his past and future. Most discussions turned to arguments and defensiveness. Communication shut down. When I pressed for conversation, matters worsened.

RELINQUISHING CONTROL

There was no going around the marital unrest; there was no denying it existed; and there was no way to write it off as another bad marriage day. We were in the eye of the storm, and the only way out was through. As the gale winds continued to gain force, I received an unexpected message from my friend Chelsea, "Remember, God is pointing the boat into the storm for a reason." She added encouragement from the Lord: "I am in control, I am driving the boat. Mary, give Me the wheel! I will guide you and guard your family. Do not fear, all will arrive safely to shore."

My anchor was unmoored, and we were drifting off to stormy seas. I had the sense the foundation of our marriage would be destroyed. Only God can raise the dead to life. Perhaps He wanted to remove the foundation of pride and put our marriage on the rock of His presence. The only hope I had was God would work all things together for our good.[9] I could cling and walk through the storm with Him, or I could lose faith and drown in the sea of despair. He was pointing us into the storm for a reason, and I would have to ride it out.

In my first marriage, I ran away. Here was the second marriage, and I was bent on obedience to God in sticking it out. After all, my role as a Christ follower was to be obedient; the results of my obedience lay in the hands of God. But relinquishing control and ownership of the results would prove almost impossible, in both the marriage and ministry. Both needed God at the helm, but I didn't know how to get out of the way. Clearly, in the school of leadership development, I was stuck in the chapter entitled, "Trusting God. His Time. His Way."

FOLLOWING CHRIST

Write the Bible reference or quote from this chapter you would like to research.

Reflections: (Reflect on what resonates with you from this chapter.)

Focus Areas: (Where do you see areas to draw closer to God?)

Actions: (What will I do this week based on my focus areas?)

Prayer: (Pen a prayer to God, inviting Him into this area of your life.)

CHAPTER 15

MY SIGNIFICANCE

*"Pleasant words are a honeycomb, sweet to the soul and
healing to the bones."* [1]

SEARCH FOR SIGNIFICANCE

Because the raging storm was intentionally designed by the enemy of
our souls (Satan) to destroy me, my family and ministry, I planted
my feet on the ground and set my face toward God's Word. If the
enemy wanted to take me down, I would give him a fight. The enemy
is deceptive and skilled at planting lies in our minds that lead us to
thoughts of being unneeded, unloved, worthless. Scripture says Satan
is the father of lies.

The first thing I would fight for was my mind. I struggled with
emotions of being insignificant, disposable, and without a voice.

Forever husband held my significance in the palm of his hand and in the words of his mouth. In trying to make him happy, I had given him control of my heart. I needed a rescue. But this time it was not a man I called upon to fill that need, it was God.

When I was a teen, I memorized scripture, "Let not your heart be troubled."[2] In previous months, God used those same words to comfort me when I couldn't sleep or when my heart ached. Could God also use scripture to silence the voices telling me I was better off dead?

I began collecting scripture to learn God's thoughts and feelings toward me. The first scripture I found provided strength for the journey toward significance. I personalize it here to demonstrate how this verse settled within my heart: "Because Mary loves Me I will rescue her. I will protect her, for she acknowledges My name. She will call upon Me, and I will answer her; I will be with her in trouble. I will deliver her and honor her. With long life I will satisfy her and show her My salvation."[3]

Through scripture, I discovered God does not criticize nor ridicule His children. He loves. He has encouraging things to say. See for yourself.

MY SIGNIFICANCE

I am made in His image. Therefore, I am enough. My life counts.
Genesis 1:27

He guards me and brings me safely to Himself.
Exodus 23:20

He looks at my heart to see my beauty.
I Samuel 16:7

I am the apple of His eye.

Psalm 17:8

He delivers me from trouble.
Psalm 50:15

He covers me with His feathers and under His wings I find refuge.
Psalm 91:4

He created me and ordered my days before I was born.
Psalm 139:13-16

I am always in His thoughts and on His mind.
Psalm 139:17-18

He knew me before I was born and He set me apart to be His child.
Jeremiah 1:5

He has good plans and a purpose for my life.
Jeremiah 29:11-13

He answers me when I call.
Jeremiah 33:3

He carries me close to His heart.
Isaiah 40:11

He holds my right hand and helps me.
Isaiah 41:13

He gives me a new heart and spirit.
Ezekiel 36:25-27

He speaks tenderly to me and leads me to a quiet place to restore me.
Hosea 2:14-15

He delights in me and rejoices over me.
Zephaniah 3:17

I am more valuable to Him than all of creation.
John 3:16

He even knows the number of hairs on my head.
Matthew 10:30

He prays for me.
Romans 8:27

He prepared me in advance to do good works.
Ephesians 2:10

He gives me strength.
Philippians 4:13

His spirit lives in me.
I Corinthians 3:16

He lavishes me with love and calls me His child.
I John 3:1

PEARLS OF DISCOVERY

I discovered the art of taking scripture and composing words of encouragement. This became a daily practice, as I knew I could not control the words spoken by others, but I could learn to control my thoughts and replace those with God's word. This exercise was key in strengthening my mind, building my confidence, and lessening the power of raw and hurtful words. Below are a few examples of these encouraging notes:

HIS IMAGE IN ME

I am created in the image of God. He designed every part of my personality, including my strengths, desires, and outward appearance.

He put within me a desire to love and to be loved. He gifted me with purpose and perseverance. If God took interest in me before my parents conceived me, doesn't that mean I have great value? He knew me before I was born. He knows the number of hairs on my head. He watches over me, prays for me, and lives in me. If this is truth, who am I to question my significance? Why allow one person (or two, or three, or four) to define who I am with their words or opinions? I am defined by God and He sees me as His treasure, His love, the apple of His eye.

PRAYER AS MY SECOND LANGUAGE

God not only hears my cries, Jesus prays for me. What better advocate can I have than God's own Son? When He speaks, it is with a gentle voice, leading me into His Presence. When I make mistakes, He does not punish me with His silence but He offers forgiveness and mercy. When I hurt, He gathers me under the shelter of His wing and loves me back to wholeness. He delivers me from trouble and carries me close to His heart.

GOD'S PERSPECTIVE

God looks at my heart and sees my motive for every action and every thought. He thinks about me all the time, and His thoughts of me are good. He delights in me and rejoices over me. He desires to spend time with me and lavishes me with love. He cares about every detail of my life, from the smallest to the overwhelming. I am His child, and He is my good Father. He put within me a purpose and a plan for my life and has called me to do good works. He never leaves my side, but is always there to hold my hand, direct my path, and help me.

REPLACING LIES WITH TRUTH

Scripture was not only a life jacket for my drowning significance; it was also the rescue in establishing truth.

At one of our Dragonfly Ministries retreat weekends, Martha talked about how we build walls around our heart to guard against emotional hurt. Though the walls may limit damage control, they also prevent the heart from freely loving God and others.

A protected heart is a lonely heart.

She used bricks to demonstrate the hardness and strength of these walls, giving names to each brick added to the stack—names like unforgiveness, rejection, abandonment, entitlement, greed, fear, and anger. She explained many bricks have been placed throughout our lives based on lies whispered by the enemy of our soul (Satan) in an attempt to shut us down and render us impotent in our life's purpose. She then suggested we list our life-lies and counter them with God-truths.

As I went into the solitude of quiet time, I journaled lies I had allowed to redirect my life, calling, purpose, and value. Then I searched scripture to find the truth countering the lies used to guard my heart. This exercise was fruitful in helping recover my sense of value and significance. I share portions of my list below:

LIE: I am disposable, of no value.

TRUTH: God loves me so much He sent His Son to die in my place.[4] God lives in me, and His love is made complete in me.[5] God knows me and loves me. He knows when I sit and when I move. He is familiar with everything about me. He is always with me, looking after me and walking with me.[6]

LIE: I cannot be a teacher; I am unable to string words together to complete a thought.

TRUTH: God's spirit in me gives me words and wisdom to speak.[7] God said to Moses, "Who gave man his mouth? Who makes him deaf or mute? Who gives him sight or makes him blind? Is it not I, the Lord? Now go; I will help you speak and will teach you what to say.[8]"

LIE: I cannot have friends because they will reject me after they come to know who I really am.

TRUTH: God tells us to love one another, for love comes from Him. He says if we love others, His love will be made complete in us. If He tells me to love others, then He also tells them to love me. I can trust He will bring people into my life to love me.[9]

LIE: My beauty comes from the outside. My weight and outward appearance are the measure of my value, and age diminishes my beauty.

TRUTH: "The Lord does not look at the things man looks at. Man looks at the outward appearance, but the Lord looks at the heart."[10] "The glory of young men is their strength; gray hair the splendor of the old."[11]

LIE: Sharing stories about everything God is doing in my life is tiresome and boring to others.

TRUTH: "Do not forget the things your eyes have seen or let them slip from your heart as long as you live. Teach them to your children and to their children after them."[12]

LIE: I am small and insignificant. I am less-than.

TRUTH: I am blessed. "Blessed are the poor in spirit, for theirs is the kingdom of heaven. Blessed are those who mourn, for they will be comforted. Blessed are the meek, for they will inherit the earth. Blessed are those who hunger and thirst for righteousness, for they will be filled." "Blessed are you when people insult you, persecute you, and falsely say all kinds of evil against you because of Me. Rejoice and be glad, because great is your reward in heaven, for in the same way they persecuted the prophets who were before you."[13]

Lord, forgive me for embracing the lies and using them as protectors of my heart. These are not what You have said of me. You said I am Your daughter, Your beloved, Your cherished one. I will love unconditionally as You teach. I will allow truth into my life. Reveal all lies that have held me captive and cover me in Your truth. Amen.

The years of studying and applying scripture were lifesavers during this season. God spoke wisdom by giving me scripture. In addition, I cannot emphasize enough the importance of acquiring the gift of recognizing God's voice and promptings. The Holy Spirit speaks truth into our spirit many times during the day. When our hearts are not tuned to Him, we miss out on His direction, guidance, and encouragement. Had I not yielded to Him during an earlier season of life, the passage through this storm would have been much more treacherous.

After this retreat weekend, my friend Beverly was so touched by the teaching on lies and truth, she decided to carry a demonstration brick home to serve as a reminder. She packed the brick into her carry-on bag which was confiscated at the airport security check-in. When airport security questioned Beverly as to why she had a brick in her carry-on bag, she took advantage of the opportunity to share Martha's lesson on dispelling the lies of Satan with the truth of scripture. Beverly made it home; the brick stayed at the airport.

FOLLOWING CHRIST

Write the Bible reference or quote from this chapter you would like to research.

Reflections: (Reflect on what resonates with you from this chapter.)

Focus Areas: (Where do you see areas to draw closer to God?)

Actions: (What will I do this week based on my focus areas?)

Prayer: (Pen a prayer to God, inviting Him into this area of your life.)

CHAPTER 16

FIGHT OR FLIGHT

*"Wrestling before God makes an impact in His kingdom. We
don't have to fight or wrestle with God, but we must wrestle
before God with things."*[1]

Wrestling before God became my exercise routine. I believed
God could bring restoration to marriage; I didn't believe God
could work a miracle in marriage. I believed God could change a
heart; I didn't believe God's plan could work with man's freewill.
It was a daily tug-of-war to walk in faith that good things come
from storms. First, one must survive the storm. I wrestled with
the questions and the outcome. Only time and obedience would
bring the answers. I was in God's school of leadership, being asked
to blindly follow the Teacher.

Confusion set in. How do I move forward, Lord? Do I stand for the marriage or flee from the trouble?[2] How do I trust You when everything I built my security on is falling apart?

SURRENDER AND TRUST

The answer came at a Dragonfly Ministries retreat weekend. During quiet time, I came upon three crosses. I laid at the foot of the center cross and prayed, "Lord, our marriage needs a resurrection. Show me Your way. Whatever You ask, I will do. We need a miracle." I sensed the presence and peace of the Holy Spirit as He asked me to trust Him. My prayer of response came quietly as I uttered these words, "May it be unto me according to Thy word."[3]

I knew this response invited God's plan into my life but also indicated heartache. It would take faith and obedience to navigate through the days ahead. Through heartbreak, God would have the opportunity to give me a new heart and reset my life. I craved a future of freedom and abundant life, set in the spacious place of God's love and presence.

In this valley of surrender a trade took place—my heart for His will.[4]

LOVE NEVER FAILS

The days of marriage grew more difficult, but it was not in me to leave. I desired to be encouraging and supportive to a man whose heart had grown cold toward me, but my resolve was weakening. I prayed,

> "Lord, I cannot do this. It is too much. If You have called me to pray forever husband through this journey, I need a fresh filling of Your love for him. My love has weakened, and I am having difficulty loving and praying for a man who has worked so hard to push me away. Help."

Immediately, an invisible heat fell over me, covering me from head to toe, as if standing in a hot shower. The sensation infiltrated my inner being, warming me through and through. God's supernatural love poured from heaven into my spirit and planted within me a deep and abiding love for forever husband. By outward appearance, nothing changed. The marriage was still in shambles. But God had given me His answer in a four-letter word. L-O-V-E.[5] I was to sacrificially love this man and show him grace at every turn.

Reprise: Obedience is not for weenies.

HIS PLAN DEFINED

Momentarily the fog lifted, and my purpose was clear. I would stand for a marriage the enemy tried to destroy with a love that could conquer this nightmare. I would walk in God's timing, which was often a long wait. My feet were planted on a rock, and God was my front and rear guard! As front guard, He would go ahead of me and prepare the way. I was to follow Him as my Commanding Officer, going and stopping as He directed. Stepping only where He stepped, speaking as He directed, and praying my family through the journey by my example of trusting God.

As rear guard, He would come behind me and hold every victory in place, so the enemy would not take the spoils of the battle. He would use my obedience as the peg to secure the victory.[6] Any ambush set against me or setback in battle would be an opportunity to reset my resolve and trust in God. He was in the undercurrent of the storm, leading me to navigate in His way, countercultural to the world around me. God opened my eyes to a new truth with new stakes. My role was obedience; His was the results.

Even if my marriage was not restored, He would use the lessons learned through my storm to speak life, understanding, and commitment into the marriages of others.

In her book, *The Overcomer's Anointing*,[7] Barbara Yoder explains, "Before God does something new with His people, He first prepares us by allowing us to go through a leveling experience in which our dependence on Him is birthed in a new way." She adds, "By our successful passage through it (the dark night of the soul), we gain a new authority over the dark night. Painful as it may be, nothing can replace the ability of the night to bring you and me through to a place of new identity, expanded power, increased influence, heightened authority and even, ultimately, honor."

Before I could help others, I had to make it through my own storm and navigate the wind and the waves in God's way. Every rocking and rowing of the boat had to come under the Master's plan. I was not to make any decisions apart from Him and I was not to speak of this journey to anyone apart from His leading.

The counsel of man would distract or deter me,
and the purpose of this storm was to teach me
His ways, so I could share the lessons with others.

THE WAY FORWARD

To write and teach about brokenness in marriage, I would be required to walk through the hardships that come when the marriage foundation crumbles, to understand the depth of dying hope, and to endure the heartbreak of forever husband walking away. Through this journey, I would gain the spiritual authority to speak wholeness and healing into the hearts and lives of those whose marriages were on the brink.

At some point in this vision, God reminded me of forever husband's free will of choice; he was not under my control or the mandate of my desires. The outcome of my standing for marriage may not produce my desired results, but my obedience to God would produce His desired outcome. I also had free will of choice. I could choose to go through this storm in a way honoring to God that would eventually help others, or I could revert to my self-centered ways and use the opportunity for vengeful or rebellious living.

A promise from God echoed in my thoughts. He had a plan and purpose for my life.[8] I would walk through this season, allowing Him to teach me His ways, so I could share the journey of hope with others.

In knowing there was a purpose for what was happening, I resolved to lean into God and stay steady, no matter what was happening in the whirlwind of life that I could physically see. I was in for the long haul, to fight for family and marriage. But not without doubt or second-guessing. The lifecycle of this storm was three-fold:

1.   Wrestling with the vision.
2.   Running from the same vision.
3.   Planting my feet back on the vision.

The revelation provided hope in the midst of the storm and reminded me to journal the lessons learned. The answer to the question "Fight or flight?" was clear. I would fight for family but at the same time, stay in flight by trusting God's perspective, living by faith rather than sight.[9]

"Write down the revelation and make it plain on tablets so that a herald may run with it. For the revelation awaits an appointed time; it speaks of the end and will not prove false. Though it linger, wait for it; it will certainly come and will not delay."[10]

Just as quickly as the fog lifted for me to see the plan for my life, it settled back even thicker, making me question that same purpose.

FOLLOWING CHRIST

Write the Bible reference or quote from this chapter you would like to research.

Reflections: (Reflect on what resonates with you from this chapter.)

Focus Areas: (Where do you see areas to draw closer to God?)

Actions: (What will I do this week based on my focus areas?)

Prayer: (Pen a prayer to God, inviting Him into this area of your life.)

CHAPTER 17

BOMB DROP AND DESTRUCTION

*"Consider it pure joy, my brothers, whenever you face trials of
many kinds, because you know that the testing of your faith
develops perseverance. Perseverance must finish its work so that
you may be mature and complete, not lacking anything."* [1]

BOMB DROP

Though my heart was filled with love for forever husband, I could not
fix him or make his struggles better. I could not clear away the debris
blocking our relationship or remove the bricks protecting his heart.
The Lord whispered, "This is not about you. Allow Me to complete
the work and stay out of My way."

I didn't know how to do that. The storm was strengthening, and the
next step would be forever husband's disappearance from my life—so

I clung to him. He felt smothered by my well-meaning, ill-placed and poorly-timed display of emotion and love. Forever husband was distant, restless, struggling, and secretive. He was a caged bird, wanting his freedom. The Lord whispered, "Open the door and let him fly."[2]

I thought setting him free meant I should make things happen. I looked for an apartment and planned to move out to give forever husband space and bring release to my crushed spirit. I thought a short separation period would fix the problem, that forever husband would wake up to the fact his family was falling apart and have a heart change. But the Lord was quick to correct. "Are you the one wanting out of the marriage?" No, Lord. "Then why are you making the decisions? Lay low and allow forever husband to make *all* decisions in this regard. Stand firm and pray."

Trying to lay low and stay out of the way proved difficult, almost impossible. Pleading with God did not produce my desired results and burying my head in the sand to avoid the truth was not progressive. My efforts failed. I could not control the outcome nor manipulate circumstances. It seemed God was forcing my surrender to gain my wholeheartedness and trust. The prayer, "May it be unto me according to Thy word" echoed in my mind, as I knew separation was inevitable and a broken marriage was not the best God had to offer. I was a prisoner of hope,[3] and this was to be done in His way and in His time.

Forever husband's way forward knocked the hope from my heart as he said, "Separation is not necessary; divorce is the only option—irreconcilable differences. No discussion, no questions, no second chances." Decision made. Forward, march.

SOLITUDE

He continued with the decision making. We sold our home and moved into separate rentals while we waited out the legal separation period. The decisions made by forever husband put me in a whirlwind of insecurity, escalated the fear of rejection, and crushed my spirit almost to death. I was in such a fog I was physically and emotionally unable to prepare for the move. God sent a friend from the faraway land of Maryland to do the packing and unpacking of possessions, and to hold me as I grieved.

I was advised by well-meaning Christians to hire an attorney, to be the first to file divorce papers, to take the lead so the court would find favor on me. Their counsel confused me. My desire was to see reconciliation of the marriage. I did not want a divorce; why would I hire an attorney? The Lord prompted me to wait. If forever husband wanted a divorce, he would initiate and lead the charge. My role was to trust, wait, and pray. My only input was to repeat these five words, "I don't want a divorce."

Immersed in brokenness and seeking emotional support, I shared with a few people my stance for marriage, believing what God joins together, no man shall separate.[4] Comments ranged from, "I can't believe you would give him a second chance," to "Just move on with your life," to "Perhaps God meant He would restore you to marry another man." Inviting others into decision making opened the door to confusion. So, I retreated inward, sharing my pain with a select few, shutting out voices contrary to my desired outcome, and taking direction only from God. The years of Dragonfly Ministries retreat quiet times had tuned my heart and spirit to recognize and hear God's voice. He had prepared me to walk through this storm; He had my ear and I had His heart.

STEPPING ASIDE FROM
DRAGONFLY MINISTRIES

In the desolate land, I held on by a thread. My spirit suffocated with a heaviness I could not bear. Forever husband's decisions hit me full throttle, and I descended into an even darker place. I didn't have the energy to carry my own pain, much less the pain of others needing a touch from God. I stepped away from Dragonfly Ministries so I could breathe again. I didn't have an exit strategy. I just stepped away. I didn't finish strong. I didn't even finish. I just stopped—and went into hibernation.

The website stalled; retreats ended, speaking engagements were cancelled. I knew I should press through and end in a way that honored the women I had grown to love. My previous failure to step away when God directed brought even more brokenness and feelings of failure. I was humbled, drained, weary, and lifeless. I had nothing left to give. The only choice I had was to crawl into the lap of Jesus and let Him breathe His life into me, bringing restoration.

And just like that, Dragonfly Ministries became a shell. It seemed everything was categorized in that same word. I was a voiceless shell with no identity. My marriage was an emotionless shell. The ministry was an empty shell. The shells were lost at sea, being tossed by the waves of a devastating storm. Would these shells indeed return safely to shore after the passage of the storm?

SEPARATION AND HEALING

The months of separation from forever husband were almost unbearable. I could not eat, and breathing was cumbersome. The pain was debilitating, with no escape. Forever husband was "moving on with his life" while I was stuck in a holding pattern, cycling between hope and shame. I leaned into God and heard His whisper,

"Hold your head high. I am here."[5]

Working at a church gave me daily access to the sanctuary. Many days, I would steal away to the balcony, out of the sight of others, and open my heart to Jesus for healing. Symbolically, I would stand with head lifted high, arms stretched out to my side, and envision Jesus nailed to the cross in front of me, trading His love for my pain.[6]

I came across a book written by Leanne Payne[7] that helped me understand what was taking place in doing this. She said when we "stand in the cross and hurt, there is a place for the pain to go—an end to it. In order to come out of pain, we must feel it. Repressed sorrow and loss remain to afflict us in other ways until we grieve them out. Stand in Christ, identify with His suffering for us, and grieve our griefs and yield up our angers, naming them and forgiving others at the same time."

This quote resurfaced many times in the days, months, and years of being made whole.[8] As I sought healing for heart wounds and a crushed spirit, I was aware I would have to re-open each wound, grieve the pain, and allow healing to come. A quick-fix, bandage grieving would not work. (By God's grace, I was not aware this journey to wholeness would encompass looking at all emotional wounds throughout my entire life, not just the ones brought on by this season.)

This deep work of grieving was the only cure for working through the pain. Often and unexpectedly, old emotional pain would return. I didn't understand why the same heartache would return, unannounced and unwelcomed. It was as if it wanted to be recognized and rewarded. In his book, *Possessing Your Inheritance*, author Chuck Pierce explains, "The process of healing from trauma and loss is a reality in life. The process of healing will go on until God's process of restoration is complete. Sometimes your pain will be revisited unexpectedly—when this happens, you know the Lord is planning to bring a deeper healing to your life. In the times of deepest pain, grace is the lifeline we must grab with both hands. As we grab on to God's grace and hope, clarity begins to come in our situation, and great comfort can sweep over us. Through this, we reach a new level of maturity. I have become aware of the power of God's grace and my need for it. My soul has grown because it has been awakened to the goodness and love of God. Loss can diminish us, but it can also expand us."[9]

The process of being made whole takes courage and resolve. It also takes time.

A HEART DIVIDED

The rollercoaster of trust and doubt highlighted a heart divided. One side hoped God would work a miracle in bringing marital reconciliation, while the other side was darkened by punishing and bitter words, holding onto a disastrous marriage, as if I owned and carried it alone.

The dark side tried to pull me under as I struggled to dethrone forever husband. I was in a pit of my own making, driven by fear and idolatry, guilty of serving two masters. It was time for one to be cut away, dethroned. Forever husband didn't want to be in my life, so the decision should be easy. But it was not. Dethroning an idol of the heart is a process. Even when the idol has turned cold.

Death held me tightly with an obsessive grip on forever husband and his choices. Yet in the back of my mind, I heard the words of Moses, as if he was speaking directly to me. "This day I call heaven and earth as witnesses against you that I have set before you life and death, blessings and curses. Now choose life, so that you and your children may live and that you may love the Lord your God, listen to His voice, and hold fast to Him. For the Lord is your life and He will give you many years in the land He swore to give to your fathers."[10]

Life was freedom from obsession and it was trusting God's ways. The choice was life. But the choice was easier to make than to walk out. Death had to be cut away,[11] and divorce would be the surgical procedure used to remove the cancerous mass of idolatry.

THE "D" WORD

The Lord prepared me that the marriage would end in divorce. This was my biggest fear, and I knew it needed to play out for my complete dependence on God to mature. Therefore, I was not surprised when the divorce papers came. Forever husband was pursuing other interests, and I was a burden he did not want to carry.

Because forever husband had filed for divorce, I was legally required to respond. My heart wrestled with disappointment and bitterness toward God. How could He allow this to happen? Were there no more miracles in His back pocket? I questioned whether I heard His voice, whether His promises were real, and if I was operating out of false hope. I emotionally crashed into the pit I had been fighting to climb out of. How was I to move forward? I had been married for twenty-five years to the same man, relocating from state to state for his career. Why would God allow this to happen? The questions prohibited me from hearing God's voice as I sat dumbfounded, trying to muster the courage to move forward.

Then I heard His gentle and loving whisper, "Stay steady."

"Are You kidding me?" I replied in anger. "For what reason?"

He asked, "Where does your hope lie?"

My heart softened as I answered, "Lord, my hope is in You. But You said You are making all things new.[12] You said You are a restorer of relationships. It feels like You have failed me, and I am a fool for believing. I will be the laughing stock of Christendom."[13]

His response, "Trust Me."[14]

Out of necessity, I found an attorney to represent me in court, but I listened to the Lord in how to proceed. I heard the gentle whisper from my Heavenly Friend, "Be as shrewd as a snake and as innocent as a dove."[15] This meant it was not my responsibility to seek revenge, yet I was to be wise in developing a plan for divorce settlement. I was to move forward in kindness and grace, allowing God to be my Defender and Provider.

> **My need for love, provision, and security was being transferred from forever husband to Eternal God.**

On January 23, the anniversary of my father's death and my sister Sandra's birthday, I sat in an Illinois courtroom across from forever husband and set him free. In the eyes of the world, he was now considered ex-husband.[16]

FLEE TO THE LAND OF PROMISE

Leaving the courthouse after the decree was signed, I found myself in a whirlwind of emotion. I called Laurie, who met me in a local parking lot and gave me a shoulder to cry on. She cried with me. With no direction or perceived purpose, I packed a suitcase, took a leave from work, and drove to Texas, where I knew the daughters would provide a safe place to heal. I returned to Illinois after a week, packed my belongings, resigned from my position with the church, and moved to Texas. "My" plan was to run from the pain and loneliness and put the brokenness behind me. (Oh, if it were that easy.) I lived with my daughter Aubrey's family. A short time after arriving, Aubrey's fifth pregnancy was met with complications, and she was put on bed rest. I cared for her family as she concentrated on protecting the pregnancy. Six weeks after the baby was born, I received a call from the church inviting me to return and help with a project. I had been in Texas four months.

When I returned to Illinois and walked into the church corridor, I was home. The staff welcomed me as a dearly loved family member. The vacant position I had left was still available, so I was re-hired. It was clear I was still in God's school of leadership, learning "the wait" of His timing for a permanent relocation to my promised land, Texas.

The land called desolate was to be where the brokenness began *and* ended. The complete work of heart healing would be done by my engagement with the staff and congregation. God used the sons, the familiarity of the job, and the church family to encourage me to "learn to live loved."[17]

Illinois is called the land of freedom. Leaving Illinois as a free woman was something only God could do, for I was still held captive by my love for forever husband. There was much work to do to set this captive free, and the Lord continued that work with two words, "Stay steady."

FOLLOWING CHRIST

Write the Bible reference or quote from this chapter you would like to research.

Reflections: (Reflect on what resonates with you from this chapter.)

Focus Areas: (Where do you see areas to draw closer to God?)

Actions: (What will I do this week based on my focus areas?)

Prayer: (Pen a prayer to God, inviting Him into this area of your life.)

CHAPTER 18

ALL THINGS NEW

"Fear not, for I have redeemed you; I have summoned you by name; you are Mine. When you pass through the waters, I will be with you, and when you pass through the rivers, they will not sweep over you. When you walk through the fire, you will not be burned; the flames will not set you ablaze. For I am the Lord your God, your Savior." [1]

STAY STEADY

After divorce, God did not release me from the covenant relationship[2] with forever husband. Even though he detached, God held me accountable to my marital vow of faithfulness. Why?

- Perhaps to continue to teach and prepare me in His ways of walking through complete forgiveness and healing in order to gain spiritual authority in speaking healing into troubled marriages. After all, spiritual authority is birthed only after brokenness has been submitted to and healed by God. My destiny is to be used of God to bring restoration to Christian marriages across our nation.

- Perhaps to bring a deeper healing and cleansing to my heart after the relational abuse I had put it through in my earlier years.

- Perhaps to prohibit me from stepping into another relationship before complete healing had come.

- Perhaps to mature me in the longsuffering process of "the wait" so I could be an encouragement to others.

- Perhaps to help someone walk through the storm with an understanding of how to navigate without wrestling or struggling with God, but with a profound faith and trust that He will keep the boat from sinking and will bring all aboard safely to the other side.

What I do understand is there are lessons learned only when we walk in obedience to His ways, rather than the ways or demands of culture. He is responsible for the results of obedience, so the burden of responsibility rests on His vast shoulders—not on mine.

THE NECESSITY OF FORGIVENESS

In standing for the marriage, the Lord gave me a mandate. I was to become a prayer warrior for forever husband, to pray for his relationships with his children, his job, and his spiritual growth. As one can imagine, my first few prayers for forever husband were not very nice, and I was a bit bitter toward God for giving me the assignment. What if I didn't want to pray for him? The Lord reminded me of the many times I needed prayer when people reached out through email, text, phone calls or in person to send me their love and let me know they were praying for me. I imagined many of those people were acting out of obedience to God in reaching out. Everyone needs a prayer warrior in their corner, including forever husband.

In my experience, wrestling before God was becoming as tiring as laying a fleece before Him. I was better off walking in obedience than trying to flee from His presence or convincing Him to change His mind. He had a knack for finding me anywhere I tried to hide.[3] So I prayed.

In carrying the mantle[4] of prayer for forever husband, I realized I harbored unforgiveness. How could I possibly pray for someone who had caused so much pain? Emotional immaturity whispered, "hold on to the hurt and punish forever husband." Spiritual maturity shouted for the better way of forgiveness.

To hold onto the hurt was to rent forever husband throne-space in my heart. He didn't want that space, so why would I freely give it to him? I was flint-faced[5] toward wholeness and healing, coupled with a desire to move forward.

**I chose to forgive, thus releasing forever husband
as the captor of my pain.**

Let me repeat four words: I chose to forgive. It was a mind decision made daily, sometimes momentarily, until it became automatic and unconditional. Forgiveness did not come overnight. It was a process. As I prayed for forever husband day after day, forgiveness moved from my mind into my heart, my attitude changed, and my emotional and mental grip loosened, bouncing me into a newfound freedom. Imagine that! God gave an assignment that brought me freedom.

THE PIT OF LONELINESS

Next in line was dealing with the pit of loneliness, the haunted house of my soul. This dark and scary place was inhabited by groaning I could not suppress or evict. I discovered extended periods of solitude fed the loneliness, and numbing the pain only increased the howling voices seeking destruction.[6] I needed new occupants, but first I had to renounce the loneliness and refuse to feed it (what we feed grows). When the loneliness and hurt returned I sat with it, felt it, and grieved through it until it disappeared. Each time, the length of the visitation was reduced, and eventually it disappeared.

At the same time, I discovered my passion for writing. I spent hours writing, and it seemed only moments passed. Writing seemed to put me in the midst of God's presence and dissipated the loneliness. I heard someone explain that destiny is a desire that won't let you go. It's more than a job. It will be a joy and will unlock creativity. This pit of loneliness had been set as an ambush to distract me, yet the healing process unlocked my destiny!

PASSION AND PURPOSE

It took a few years after the divorce for a passion for life to return as I accepted the challenge to discover the woman God designed me to be. I was called to follow Him regardless of the opinions, control, or voices of others seeking to occupy space on the throne of my heart. This was my second chance.

Slowly, newness found its way into the days. Smiles turned to laughter. Loneliness turned to serving others. Heartache turned to lessons, and the past storm turned into a deeper discovery of God and self and began making its way out of my heart onto paper.

For years, the enemy's attempt to silence and render me unfruitful appeared successful. Dragonfly Ministries was all but dead, save a website that hosted a banner saying, "under construction." It was as empty and bare-boned as I was. I appreciated the break in life, as I needed space to "just be." But in the silence and darkness, God reversed the enemy's tactics and attempts to destroy and silence me to make me stronger. Step by step, God directed my path. Day by day, He brought restoration and healing.

"God's heart is always to restore, to bring back to life, to reinstate, rebuild, reestablish, renovate, and repair." [7]

REBUILDING

During the sixth year of employment with the church, I sensed the winds of change. This time, the gentle breeze alerted me that it was time to go home. In preparation for the move, I was to "finish strong" in my position. I did not want to repeat the "just quit" method, as I had done with Dragonfly Ministries, or the "run away" method when I fled to Texas immediately after the divorce.

I developed an exit strategy, defining roles and responsibilities to backfill for a smooth transition, and I dug my heels in to finish on a strong note. After seven years of employment, I returned home to my land of miracles and ministry. This time, I wasn't running away from anything; rather I was running forward. Symbolically, I donated furniture and household items so the load taken to Texas would be light. Starting over would not include weighted memories housed in fixtures from the past. This was a time for "the new."

To my surprise, "the new" included many memories of family and friends in Illinois. Memories of laughter, hugs, dinners and movies, shopping sprees, and Friday nights. The land I called desolate turned out to be my land of freedom.[8] For in that land, God took my brokenness and brought me into a spacious place of purpose. He surrounded me with church staff to love me to wholeness. He increased the bond of love and devotion between me and the sons and daughters. And He showed me that once I stopped running from the pain, it stopped chasing me. When I gave Him my past to bury, I saw my clear destiny ahead, this time without the fog. And I understood overcoming the burdens of yesterday are the wings that fly me through my tomorrows.

At the time of this writing, my time in Texas has been less than a year. In that period, I have completed the writing of this first book and am working on the second. I have enjoyed much time with the daughters and their families, and I have traveled back several times to the land of freedom to visit the sons (now grown and "adulting") and my Midwest friends. I feel compelled to give more details of my rebuilt life, but that will require time, for time must write the story before I can tell it. And as I close this chapter of my life story, I again sense the gentle winds of change blowing, bringing the fragrance of God's kindness, and the days ahead are filled with hope!

FOLLOWING CHRIST

Write the Bible reference or quote from this chapter you would like to research.

Reflections: (Reflect on what resonates with you from this chapter.)

Focus Areas: (Where do you see areas to draw closer to God?)

Actions: (What will I do this week based on my focus areas?)

Prayer: (Pen a prayer to God, inviting Him into this area of your life.)

CHAPTER 19

THE TREASURES OF DARKNESS

"I will give you the treasures of darkness,
riches stored in secret places." [1]

VICTORY

"God gets His greatest victories out of apparent defeats.
Very often the enemy seems to triumph a little, and God
lets it be so; but then He comes in and upsets all the work
of the enemy, overthrows the apparent victory, and as the
Bible says, "turns the way of the wicked upside down."
Thus, He gives a great deal larger victory than we would
have known if He had not allowed the enemy, seemingly,
to triumph in the first place. Do not own a great trial as a
defeat, but continue, by faith, to claim the victory through
Him who is able to make you more than a conqueror, and

a glorious victory will soon be apparent. He is making opportunities for us to exercise faith in Him as will bring about blessed results and greatly glorify His name."[2]

STORM AFTERMATH

I have seen midlife spouses come home during and after their crisis. God has given me voice to speak hope and faith to spouses who desire to stand for their marriage. Be encouraged to weather the storm in your life. Step on the obstacles blocking your way and turn them into stepping stones. Do it God's way and in His timing, so He goes ahead of you to prepare the way and comes behind you as your rear guard. In His way, you will be able to see God stake your progress so you can press forward. His ways keep you from moving backwards.

"It is in the storm of life that God equips us for service. When God wants an oak, He plants it on the moor where the storms will shake it and the rains will beat down upon it, and it is in the midnight battle with elements that the oak wins its rugged fiber and becomes the king of the forest. When God wants to make a man, He puts him into some storm. The history of mankind is always rough and rugged. No man is made until he has been out into the surge of the storm and found the sublime fulfillment of the prayer, "O God, take me, break me, make me." The beauties of nature come after the storm. The rugged beauty of the mountain is born in a storm, and the heroes of life are the storm-swept and battle-scarred."[3]

BEING ONE-DIMENSIONAL

I am a Jesus follower living a life of adventure in a real world; I am 3-D. But my values and views of Christ are one-dimensional, and of that, I am not ashamed. Psalm 25 teaches what being one-dimensional means.

- I am aware of the abiding presence of God always.
- I walk in the ways of the Lord and am guided by His truth.
- I am personally taught by God and trust wholeheartedly in Him.
- I seek forgiveness for past and current sin.
- I seek to be made new.
- I hold the Lord's confidence.
- I love, respect, and honor the Lord.
- I look to the Lord in all things.
- God is my rescue, hope, and refuge.
- My one-dimensional life means I am hemmed in by God, confident of His protection and provision. I live with the spiritual companions of love, peace, trust, and contentment.
- I am called to live and move and have my being in God, from the inside out.[4]

THE MAKING OF A DRAGONFLY

"As water reflects a face, so a man's heart reflects the man."[5]

On my final day working with the church, I argued against a going-away party. I knew the departure would be emotional, and I didn't want the floodgate of tears to break in full view of my dearly beloved staff. Moving away from the sons was hard enough, and I knew the grieving tears would accompany me half-way to Texas. Departure is always bittersweet.

The staff somewhat ignored my wishes, but I give full credit (or blame) to God. He knew that the sentiments of staff would push me through the hard days of relocating.[6] He knew I needed the revelation that, even when I was not aware, His aroma escaped through my love for and service to others.

As we gathered for a "departmental meeting," staff members shared how my journey made a lasting spiritual impact in their lives. They spoke of how my love for and obedience to God were personal life changers. They spoke of how my leaning into God rather than the counsel of man redirected their personal decision making. They spoke of the love I shared with others by my willingness to pray and sit with those who were hurting. Through the task of walking through the darkness and storm, somehow, I was able to stop striving to be a Jesus follower and just metamorphosed into being.

And in "just being," God used me as His dragonfly to absorb His love and shine it out for others to see. Without striving to be a Christian, without being burdened to live so others would see His light, it happened anyway. I guess what is in the heart is truly reflected.

For God, who said, "Let light shine out of darkness," made His light shine in our hearts to give us the light of the knowledge of the glory of God in the face of Christ."[7]

We are called to reflect God's love in a darkened world. Will you be a dragonfly for God?

FOLLOWING CHRIST

Write the Bible reference or quote from this chapter you would like to research.

Reflections: (Reflect on what resonates with you from this chapter.)

Focus Areas: (Where do you see areas to draw closer to God?)

Actions: (What will I do this week based on my focus areas?)

Prayer: (Pen a prayer to God, inviting Him into this area of your life.)

CHAPTER 20

CONCLUSION AND PRAYER FOR FAMILIES

"Blessed are all who fear the Lord, who walk in His ways." [1]

STUDENT OF THE LORD

My greatest burden in sharing my story is in trying to reconcile why I would walk through this storm and not see the marriage with forever husband restored. The story almost didn't make it to paper or print. Perhaps my story will bring discouragement to those who are trusting God to rekindle their marriage. Or perhaps sharing a story without the "fairy tale happy ending" will be a letdown to those who have read through the chapters anticipating forever husband to ride in and save the damsel in distress. But perhaps, a real-life story of faith, fear, disappointment, and discovery in the midst of a storm will bring hope to those who have suffered loss and hope has vanished.

The Lord placed a fire in me to fight with all I had to save my marriage as a display of His power. I walked through the pain with hope and learned how to walk through marital conflict, strife, separation, and divorce in His way. I chose and choose to believe God's promises to bring restoration and reconciliation to broken marriages. Though my marriage has not been restored, I truly believe God will work through my obedience and experience to bring healing to many marriages. It has been worth the heartbreak and pain to see marriages saved, even as I walked through the demise.

The enemy had a plan in place to destroy me and render me silent. But his plan backfired. During my stormy season, God used my pain and brokenness to teach me how to battle for marriages. The years of traversing through trails of tears, prayer, brokenness, surrender, and sacrifice has given hope to others willing to walk the hard journey of standing and fighting for their marriage and family. I can truly say, "What the enemy meant for harm has been reversed to be used of God to bring glory to His name."[2]

He used the darkness to cause me to search, to seek, to cry out for healing and wholeness. Through the darkness of the destruction of marriage, He gave me a heart for families, for marriages, for helping others navigate through this storm in a way that brings glory and honor to God and leaves them without regret, resentment or fear. God can help them step on the fears and turn them into stepping stones, creating a pathway forward.

As the evening primrose blooms only in the dark, God used darkness to bring me to full bloom.

PRAYER FOR FAMILIES

Father, thank You for the spouse committed to stand for their marriage, not willing to give in to social, cultural or worldly pressure or ideals that "divorce is the only option" or "happiness is more important than family and honor." Steel the feet of those who stand for healing in their marriages, who stand for marriage restoration and reconciliation.

Pour into them a spiritually deep love for their forever spouse and remind them daily of Your promise of faithfulness and Your love for the entity of marriage. ("For this reason, a man will leave his father and mother and be united to his wife, and the two will become one flesh. So they are no longer two, but one. Therefore what God has joined together, let man not separate." Matthew 19:6.)

Infuse Your perseverance in their stand, Lord. Provide mentors to walk and pray them through this journey. May You be the God of their heart. May they find their identity in You and may their destiny come forth as they stand. Refine their character, Lord, and guard their heart. May they seek Your heart and Your ways at every decision, every point. May they come to You for answers and direction.

Father, we lift to You the forever husband and forever wife who struggles to honor their covenant vow with You and their standing spouse. We pray, Lord, that You give them shoes of peace so the fog of confusion and deception is lifted and they journey home where they are loved.

We bind Satan's attempts to destroy marriages in our nation, Lord, and we declare to You the desire to see marriages restored, reconciled. We desire, Lord, to see marriages built on the foundation of You. Heal the forever spouse, Lord. Heal marriages, Lord. May love prevail; love for You and love for family. May we keep no record of wrongs,

Lord, but may the forever spouse be led, with kindness and prayer, back into the family, with arms wide open. Lord, make a way where there seems to be no way. Hold the hearts pure and ready to receive the wayward spouse back into their rightful place in their family.

We commit our way unto You, Father. Be honored in the stand for godly and strong marriages. We look forward to Your work in the lives of marriages and families across this great nation. Be honored, Lord, and may Your name be praised.

In the precious name of Jesus Christ our Lord we pray,

Amen.

ABOUT THE AUTHOR

Mary Ethel Eckard is an ordained minister and founder of Dragonfly Ministries–dedicated to the spiritual growth and encouragement of women. She travels internationally to speak and teach at women's conferences, workshops, and retreats. She has a heart for teaching women how to pursue God and walk in His ways. Her captivating testimony chronicles a journey of relying on God's strength and guidance to navigate the storms and dark days of life–coming out on the other side with a greater maturity in and intimacy with Christ.

Mary's chief calling is to reflect God's light, joy, and love so that others will be drawn to Him—the source of life—as referenced in

Matthew 5:16: *"Let your light shine before men, that they may see your good deeds and praise your Father in heaven."*

www.MaryEthelEckard.com

www.DragonflyMinistries.com

INVITE MARY TO YOUR NEXT EVENT

If you would like to schedule Mary to speak at your event, please contact her at: Admin@MaryEthelEckard.com or through her website at MaryEthelEckard.com.

ENDNOTES

Foreword

1. 1 Corinthians 15:55 (NLT)

This Book as a Study Tool

1. Psalm 91:1 (NKJV)

Introduction

1. Isaiah 61:3

2. 2 Corinthians 1:3-4

3. Psalm 91:1, 4

4. Psalm 17:8

Chapter 1

1. Jeremiah 1:5

2. The Ten Commandments, Exodus 20:1-17

3. The phrase "me-mode" reminds me of commode, which is pretty much where I managed to park my life for this season.

4. Judges 6:37-39

Chapter 2

1. Zechariah 1:3

2. Matthew 6:24: "No one can serve two masters. Either you will hate the one and love the other, or you will be devoted to the one and despise the other."

3. Becca LaBar says, "Jesus freak is a compliment. People who revolve their lives around Jesus are often looked down upon, ridiculed, and judged. So, if someone calls you a Jesus freak, be happy about it. Take the name as a little note from God that you are doing something right. If you are living your life in a way that shows God's love and light so much that you get a nickname about it, keep doing what you're doing." LaBar, Becca. "I'm a 'Jesus Freak' and I'm Proud," Accessed 5 January 2017. https://www.theodysseyonline.com/jesus-freak-and-proud. Accessed 3 October 2017.

4. Matthew 12:34: "Out of the overflow of the heart the mouth speaks."

5. Psalm 51:3, 7, 10

6. I John 5:14-15

Chapter 3

1. Isaiah 55:9

2. Patty Zemanick Williams is the author of a children's book entitled *A Walk with Papa*, published by Dragonfly Ministries. She has also authored a children's play, *I'm a Child of God*. Patty lives in upstate New York with her husband John. They are the parents of six children.

3. This is not how Patty got her nickname as a holy roller, though it would aptly apply.

4. Blackaby, Henry and King, Claude V., *Experiencing God: Knowing and Doing the Will of God,* Nashville: B&H Publishing Group, 2008. (Knowing God does not come through a program, a study, or a method. Knowing God comes through a relationship with a Person. This is an intimate love relationship with God. Through this relationship, God reveals Himself, His purposes, and His ways; and He invites you to join Him where He is already at work.)

5. Did you count to make sure there were eight words?

6. Often, people ask how to know if what they are hearing is from God. I suggest they measure what they are hearing against scripture. If it aligns with scripture and/or if it is an act of kindness and love, move forward. Even if it was not God's promptings, you have done something nice for another person, and scripture says we are to love others.

7. Judges 6:37-39, further explained in Chapter 1 endnotes. Laying a fleece before God was the way I became more familiar with hearing God's voice and promptings. After a season, I no longer used this method because my spirit became more opened to God.

8. The kidney transplant took place before being a living donor was a common procedure.

Chapter 4

1. I John 2:6

2. When our Christianity is based on the revelations God gives others, rather than to us, we limit our capacity and ability to know God at an intimate level.

3. Chambers, Oswald, "October 23," *My Utmost for His Highest,* Edited by James Reimann, Grand Rapids: Discovery House Publishers, 1992.

4. I use this term loosely. A better word may be 'attention'. I was never asked for an autograph, the paparazzi didn't follow me, and I didn't sign a movie deal.

5. Luke 14:25-35, Matthew 10:26-39

6. Cultural Christianity is one who claims to be a Christian without allowing Jesus Christ to be personal Lord of her life.

7. Newton-John, Olivia, "Let Me Be There," written by John Rostill, *Let Me Be There,* MCA Records, 1973.

8. Exodus 4:11

9. Mark 13:11

Chapter 5

1. Psalm 33:11

2. Chambers, Oswald, "October 11," *My Utmost for His Highest,* Edited by James Reimann, Grand Rapids: Discovery House Publishers, 1992.

3. Galatians 1:15

4. TerKuerst, Lisa, "If You Ever Feel Lonely, Read This," 21 July 2016, http://www.Proverbs31.org/devotions. Accessed 6 November 2017.

5. Luke 15:4-6

6. Again, a bit dramatic but it was the way I was feeling, and vulnerability in sharing this is important here.

7. In my baby state of following Christ, I had not yet learned to discern His voice or presence. My elementary way of seeking God was in laying out a fleece, asking Him to give me a sign to show me His answer. In His grace and love, He answered in this way as I was also learning to recognize and discern His voice

and promptings. He wants us to see and know Him and seeking His heart through laying out a fleece is not wrong. In later years, God corrected this practice in me by saying, "We are past the fleece prayers. Either you trust me or you don't. Do not seek my will through this method anymore. I will not respond." Also see footnote on fleeces in Chapter 1.

8. As I explained earlier, praying out loud has been effective for me because once I hear the words leave my lips, I wait expectantly for the answer. Psalm 139:4 says "Before a word is even on my tongue, God knows it." Isaiah 65:24 says, "Before they call I will answer; while they are still speaking, I will hear." It is comforting that God knows what we need before we ask and has often put the answer into motion even before we speak our request to Him.

9. I learned about perseverance through Jacob, when He held onto the Lord and wrestled all night until he was given the blessing he desired. This story is told in Genesis 32:22-32.

10. To understand God's true value of His creation, study Psalm 139. He treasures His children. The enemy, Satan, works to tell us otherwise so we veer off course in our destiny. My destiny had been diverted by the enemy for years and my heart's cry was to stay on God's path rather than allowing distractions to again intervene.

11. My theology was wrong. Many of my beliefs about God had been sculpted from my experience with humans. God forgives and restores. He is good, and all that He does is good. Even while stalling, His answer produced a hunger in me to persevere.

12. God loves us in many ways. He speaks through His creation— through the sunrise and sunset, through the formation and movement of the clouds, through the song of a bird, the flowers in a field, the rain and storms. God is not offended when we ask

Him to make Himself known. He desires to be known, to shower us with His love and His direction. Invite Him into your life; don't be afraid to ask Him to reveal Himself to you.

Chapter 6

1. Isaiah 55:10-11

2. God is always at work behind the scenes, orchestrating our lives and preparing us for the next thing. Amid these periods of restlessness, we need to lean into Him and stay available to what He is bringing into our lives. Don't fill life with busyness and miss out on His best.

3. In the *Experiencing God* study, Henry Blackaby explains that one of the ways God speaks is through scripture. I knew it was not my responsibility to convict or save these women because that job belongs to God. I also knew by opening scripture, they would have the opportunity of a lifetime.

4. John 8:47

Chapter 7

1. Lamentations 3:22-23

2. Habakkuk 2:2: "Then the Lord answered me and said: Write the vision; make it plain on tablets, so that a runner may read it. For there is still a vision for the appointed time; it speaks of the end and does not lie. If it seems to tarry, wait for it; it will surely come, it will not delay.

3. Cowman, Mrs. Charles E., "October 28," *Streams in the Desert,* Grand Rapids: Zondervan, 1997.

Chapter 8

1. Psalm 119:105

2. Hosea 2:14-15

3. I John 2:27

4. Matthew 6:25-31

5. Psalm 32:6-7

6. Proverbs 3:5-6

7. John 8:11 (KJV)

Chapter 9

1. Hebrews 12:1-2

2. Patty, the Holy Roller

3. Psalm 40:2

4. I Corinthians 13:11

5. See Chapter 4, *The Second Chance*

6. Martha Shipman

7. Jennifer Eitel Young

Chapter 10

1. I Samuel 3:9

2. It's the raw, selfish truth.

3. Psalm 139:1

4. I Kings 19:19-21

Chapter 11

1. Psalm 46:10

2. Amos 3:7 teaches that the Lord prepares us for what is to come; we just need to have our spirit open to Him so we are aware of His preparation.

3. Romans 8:28

4. Dad passed on January 23 of that year. On a lighter note, it's also my sister Sandra's birthday.

5. 2 Timothy 1:12

6. When my friend Jan needs a good cry, she draws a tub of hot water, lights a few candles, soaks in the steamy water, and cries. She has great traditions. She also keeps her toenails unpolished between the months of October and March to give them a break. Where would we be without girlfriends!

7. 2 Corinthians 12:9

8. A church member, Miss Margaret, shared with me, "I have been praying for years for someone to come and lead our women's ministry. You are an answer to that prayer." Her heart for God and for the women of the church humbled me. My desire was to be used of God to point the women's hearts toward God.

9. Sanctuary is defined as "a place of refuge or safety; a consecrated place."

10. I may have just invented a new phrase: "hair rebellion." This is when a son decides he doesn't want the clean-cut hair anymore; he wants to look like a rock star. This has caused angst in more than one family through the generations.

11. During this season, we were introduced to new forms of music that sounded nothing like Celine Dion, Willie Nelson, or Michael W. Smith.

12. *A Walk with Papa*, written by Patty Zemanick, the holy roller, and illustrated by Sandra Hammack, my sister.

Chapter 12

1. 2 Corinthians 4:17-18

2. A southern saying meaning "stand your ground."

3. Ruth 1:16

4. I Corinthians 13

5. Numbers 6:24-26

6. Déjá vu

Chapter 13

1. Jeremiah 6:16

2. Psalm 16:11

3. Matthew 12:33-37

4. This is the title of a book: Christenson, Evelyn, *Lord, Change Me,* Scripture Press, 1968. In the book, she prays, "Lord, change me—not my husband, not my children, don't change my pastor, but change me." My mom gave me a copy of this book years earlier and it had made a great impact on my spiritual journey.

5. Pierce, Chuck D., "Foreword." *The Overcomer's Anointing,* by Barbara J. Yoder, Grand Rapids: Chosen Books, 2009.

6. John 3:16

7. Isaiah 42:16

Chapter 14

1. Exodus 23:20

2. For the next seven years, I was part of this church staff. At the end of the seven-year period, the Lord released me to return to Texas, where I would step into new life with ministry and book writing. He used this lighthouse to teach me and grow me into a true ministry leader.

3. Still today, my desire is to tell how God walked me through this storm without dishonoring forever husband.

4. I Corinthians 13:7

5. "The Hallmarks of the Midlife Crisis," *The Heart's Blessings Presents Series,* https://thestagesandlessonsofmidlife.org/the-hallmarks-of-the-mid-life-crisis. Accessed 7 February 2018. Their websites walked me through what was happening with forever husband and helped me regain confidence in who God had created me to be as well as healing through the anger and emotional outbursts that were a part of forever husband's journey through midlife. These websites are written from a Christian perspective and helped me realize great spiritual and emotional truths, specifically that I could not control nor help forever husband through his journey; my role was to allow God to heal me and to pray him through.

6. Jim Conway was a pioneer in writing about midlife crisis; his book *Midlife Crisis in Men* is a great introductory tool of what this season of life involves. Conway, Jim and Sally. *Midlife Crisis in Men.* Cook Communications, 1985.

7. "The Stages and Lessons of Midlife," *The Heart's Blessings Presents Series,* http://Thestagesandlessonsofmidlife.org. Accessed 7 February 2018; and *Welcome to the Hero's Spouse,* http://www.midlifecrisismarriageadvocate.com. Accessed 7 February 2018.

8. "Crisis," *Merriam Webster.com,* https://www.merriam-webster. com/dictionary/crisis. Accessed 7 February 2018.

9. Romans 8:28

Chapter 15

1. Proverbs 16:24

2. John 14:1-3 (KJV)

3. Psalm 91:14

4. John 3:16

5. I John 4:10-12

6. Psalm 139

7. Luke 21:15

8. Exodus 4:11-12

9. I John 4:7

10. I Samuel 16:7

11. Proverbs 20:29

12. Deuteronomy 4:9

13. Matthew 5:3-6, 11-12

Chapter 16

1. Chambers, Oswald, "December 16," *My Utmost for His Highest,* Edited by James Reimann, Grand Rapids: Discovery House Publishers, 1992.

2. Hosea 2:14-15. God promises to make the valley of trouble a door of hope.

3. Luke 1:38. Mary's response to the angel Gabriel when He spoke

to her about birthing the Messiah.

4. 2 Corinthians 5:21 God made Him (Jesus) who had no sin to be sin for us, so that in Him we might become the righteousness of God. This was the greatest trade of all time.

5. I Corinthians 13:4-8, "Love is patient, love is kind. It does not envy, it does not boast, it is not proud. It is not rude, it is not self-seeking, it is not easily angered, it keeps no record of wrongs. Love does not delight in evil but rejoices with the truth. It always protects, always trusts, always hopes, always perseveres. Love never fails."

6. Isaiah 22:23

7. Yoder, Barbara J. *The Overcomer's Anointing,* Grand Rapids: Chosen Books, 2009. 42.

8. Jeremiah 29:11-13

9. 2 Corinthians 5:7

10. Habakkuk 2:2-3

Chapter 17

1. James 1:2-4

2. I do not believe divorce was God's plan, but I do believe I needed to stop clinging, and God knew my crushed spirit needed to be healed. I needed to release forever husband to his own journey and trust God with the outcome.

3. Zechariah 9:13, "Return to your fortress, O prisoners of hope; even now I announce that I will restore twice as much to you."

4. Matthew 19:6

5. Psalm 3:3-4, "But you are a shield around me, O Lord; you bestow glory on me and lift up my head. To the Lord I cry aloud,

and He answers me from his holy hill."

6. Isaiah 53:5, "He was pierced for our transgressions, He was crushed for our iniquities; the punishment that brought us peace was upon hHm, and by His wounds we are healed."

7. Payne, Leanne, *The Healing Presence: Curing the Soul through Union with Christ*, Grand Rapids: Baker Books, 1989. 205-206.

8. "A Biblical Definition of "Wholeness"—The state of being perfectly well in body, soul (mind, will and emotions) and spirit. Complete sanctification and restoration. *Wholeness: A Biblical and Christian Perspective.* http://www.faithandhealthconnection. org/the_connection/spirit-soul-and-body/wholeness-biblical-and-christian-perspective/ Accessed 7 February 2018.

9. Pierce, Chuck and Rebecca Sytsema, *Possessing Your Inheritance*, Grand Rapids: Chosen Books, 2009.

10. Deuteronomy 30:19-20

11. Romans 8:5-8

12. Revelation 21:5

13. A little dramatic and overstated, but unmet expectations and flailing emotions do that to a girl.

14. One grows weary in the recognition that the sword of trust in the Creator of the Universe, the One who designed humans and has a plan for each life, is still not wielded. "Lord, increase my faith." Luke 17:5

15. Matthew 10:16

16. Our marriage lasted for 25 years, but that does not equal forever. I share my story with you through the lens of God's perspective after years of seeking Him and understanding His ways. Though the marriage to forever husband ended, the impact of lessons learned due to the marriage and breakup are eternal. God gave

me the treasures of darkness as He taught and matured me in ways that would not have been reached without the heartbreak that ensued when the marriage ended. Some have asked me to change the phrase to ex-husband; you can see I did not. God used this man in a significant way to challenge and redirect my life, which is an eternal life in Christ, which means forever.

17. A phrase coined by my dear friend, Susie Bell, HCL Ministries.

Chapter 18

1. Isaiah 43:1-3

2. God considers marriage a holy covenant.

3. Psalm 139 says I can't flee from His presence. That didn't stop me from trying to hide.

4. God assigned me to the responsibility of praying for forever husband; mantle is another way to say responsibility.

5. Isaiah 5:7, "Because the Sovereign Lord helps me, I will not be disgraced. Therefore, have I set my face like flint, and I know I will not be put to shame."

6. John 10:10, Jesus said, "The thief comes only to steal and kill and destroy; I have come that they may have life, and have it to the full."

7. Yoder, Barbara J., *The Overcomer's Anointing*, Grand Rapids: Chosen Books, 2009.

8. Illinois is called "The Land of Freedom"

Chapter 19

1. Isaiah 45:3

2. Cowman, Mrs. Charles E., "January 18," *Streams in the Desert*,

Grand Rapids: Zondervan, 1997.

3. Cowman, Mrs. Charles E., "January 16," *Streams in the Desert,* Grand Rapids: Zondervan, 1997.

4. Acts 17:28

5. Proverbs 27:19

6. The sons stayed in the Illinois/Wisconsin region, as well as sweet friendships that would be tested by distance.

7. 2 Corinthians 4:6

Chapter 20

1. Psalm 128:1

2. This reminds me of the story of Joseph found in the book of Genesis. Joseph's brothers sold him into slavery because they were jealous of him. He served for many years in Egypt and was eventually put in charge of the whole land of Egypt. When Joseph was governor of the land, a great famine came. Joseph's brothers came to Egypt to buy grain and when they learned the Governor of the land was their own brother whom they had sold into slavery, they were afraid that he would kill them. Instead, Joseph's response was profound and filled with grace. He told them, "You intended to harm me, but God intended it for good to accomplish what is now being done, the saving of many lives."

WORKS CITED

Unless otherwise noted, all scripture quotations are from the NIV.

The Bible. New King James Version. New York: Harper Collins, 1982.

The Bible. New Living Translation. Carol Stream: Tyndale House, 2005.

The Bible. Zondervan NIV Life Application Study Bible. Grand Rapids: Zondervan, 1984.

Blackaby, Henry and King, Claude V. *Experiencing God: Knowing and Doing the Will of God.* Nashville: B&H Publishing Group, 2008.

Chambers, Oswald. *My Utmost for His Highest.* Edited by James Reimann. Grand Rapids: Discovery House Publishers, 1992.

Christenson, Evelyn. *Lord, Change Me.* Scripture Press, 1968.

Conway, Jim and Sally. *Midlife Crisis in Men.* Cook Communications Ministries International. 1985.

Cowman, Mrs. Charles E. *Streams in the Desert.* Grand Rapids: Zondervan, 1997.

"Crisis." *Merriam-Webster.com.* Updated 20 January 2018. http://www.meriam-webster.com/dictionary/crisis. Accessed January 23, 2018.

"The Hallmarks of the Midlife Crisis." *The Heart's Blessings Presents*

Series. https://thestagesandlessonsofmidlife.org/the-hallmarks-of-the-mid-life-crisis. Accessed 7 February 2018.

Hearts Blessing. *The Hallmarks of the Midlife Crisis.* https://thestagesandlessonsofmidlife.org/the-hallmarks-of-the-mid-life-crisis/. Assessed date October 27, 2017.

King James Version. BibleGateway.com, 1987. https://www.biblegateway.com/versions/King-James-Version-KJV-Bible.

LaBar, Becca. "Jesus Freak and Proud." 5 January 2017. http://www.odysseyonline.com/jesus-freak-and-proud. Accessed 3 October 2017.

Newton-John, Olivia. "Let Me Be There," written by John Rostill. *Let Me Be There* MCA Records, 1973.

Payne, Leanne. *The Healing Presence: Curing the Soul through Union with Christ.* Baker Books, 1989.

Pierce, Chuck D. "Foreword." *The Overcomer's Anointing,* by Barbara J. Yoder. Grand Rapids: Chosen Books, 2009.

Pierce, Chuck. *Possessing Your Inheritance.* Grand Rapids: Chosen Books, 2009.

Ruth, Kenda, The Hero's Spouse. www.midlifecrisismarriageadvocate.com. Assessed September 2012.

"The Stages and Lessons of Midlife." *The Heart's Blessings Presents Series.* http://Thestagesandlessonsofmidlife.org. Accessed 7 February 2018

TerKeurst, Lysa. "If You Ever Feel Lonely, Read This." 21 July 2016. https://proverbs31.org/devotions. Accessed 6 November 2017.

Welcome to the Hero's Spouse, http://www. midlifecrisismarriageadvocate.com. Accessed 7 February 2018.

Yoder, Barbara. *The Overcomer's Anointing.* Grand Rapids: Chosen Books,2009.

Zemanick, Patty. *A Walk With Papa.* Dallas: Dragonfly Ministries Publication, 2007.

Made in the USA
Lexington, KY
09 May 2018